INFILTRATION

INFILTRATION

By

Bishop Ukaegbu Ogwo

Copyright © 2004 by Ukaegbu Ogwo
First Revision Copyright © 2017
Published in USA by: Createspace (an Amazon company)

Bishop Ukaegbu Ogwo
Mountain Height Assembly
16 Howell's Crescent,
P.O. Box 4674 Aba,
Zip code: 450001,
Abia State, Nigeria
Tel.: 234 803 323 4516
E-mail: rev@solartimeelectric.net

No part of this book may be reproduced, stored in any retrieval system or transmitted in any form or by any means electronic, mechanical, electrostatic, magnetic tape, photocopy or otherwise, without the due written permission of the author, being the copyright owner.

ISBN: 978-978-917-467-6

The Bible texts in this publication, unless otherwise indicated, are from the New King James Version (NKJV). Copyright © 1979, 1980, 1982, Thomas Nelson, Inc. Publishers.

Contents

		Page #
Table of Contents		
Dedication		5
Acknowledgement		6
Preface		8
Chapter 1	***Speaking in Tongues***	21
Chapter 2	***"Slain" Under Anointing***	53
Chapter 3	***Misdirected Militancy***	78
Chapter 4	***Undue Exaltation of the Devil***	114
Chapter 5	***Present-day Misuse of the Old Covenant***	145
Chapter 6	***Who is Exalted, You or God?***	206
Chapter 7	***Prophetic Deception***	219

Dedication

This book is dedicated to my beloved wife ***Ivu***, the undisputed help meet for me, who has no need to impress in order to be appreciated.

Acknowledgements

I acknowledge that the seed thought to write this book came from a discussion I had with my beloved brother Ndubuisi Ogwuama of the Nigerian Bank for Commerce and Industry (NBCI) in Lagos in November 1993. We were both grieved in the spirit over the ever-increasing digression of the Church from laid down Bible principles. As we were sharing our experiences and feelings on this subject, the Holy Spirit spoke to me instructing that I should write this book. I shared the impression with Brother Ogwuama and he encouraged me in the endeavor.

In less than one month the whole book, except the last chapter, was written. After six months, the Holy Spirit again spoke to me to publish the book or He would raise others to publish the same material He gave me. The material contents of the book appeared so controversial to me, at that time, that I was actually scared to publish them. But by late 1995, I read a book by Dr. David Oyedepo of Living Faith Church, published that same year which contained some of the materials of my unpublished book.

With the encouragement that this great man of God shared the same thoughts that I was afraid to publish, I went ahead and wrote the last chapter ***Prophetic Deceptions*** in April 1996. This chapter was also paraphrased as a tract. Then I reviewed the entire manuscript for publication.

I also wish to acknowledge the help of my wife Gloria Ivuarulam Ogwo who organized and edited the manuscript. Pastor Luke Ukachukwu, the Overseer of The Victory Assembly Aba, Abia State, Nigeria, my prayer partner at that time, assisted in editing the last chapter of the book. Lastly, I acknowledge the dedication of Miss Eunice Onyedire of Prispaul Nigeria Ltd., Aba who painstakingly saw the typesetting of the manuscript to a successful qualitative finish. May the Lord Jesus Christ reward you all for your varied contributions in this work of His vineyard?

PREFACE

It is pathetic to see that in the on-going battle between the Church of Jesus Christ and the kingdom of darkness, the Church has been dealt some very terrible blows in this end time. Yet she is ignorant of this.

> ***My people are destroyed for lack of knowledge, Hosea 4-6.***

This word is truer today than it has ever been. The Lord Jesus Christ warned us about this attack as part of the end-time prophecies.

> ***Then many false prophets will rise up and deceive many. And because lawlessness will abound the love of many will grow cold. For false Christs and false prophets will rise and show great signs and wonders, so as to deceive, if possible, even the elect. Matt. 24:11-12, 24***

Paul the apostle was also used by the Holy Spirit to warn us who are of this end-time generation, 2Thess 2:3, and 2:7a, 9-12

Apostle Peter spoke in particular detail about the coming of false teachers. Chapter two of the book of Second Peter deals with this issue, 2Peter 2:1.

The apostle was prophesying then, that the Church was going to be invaded by false teachers. At the time of this prophecy, there were already false prophets. But Peter said that the false teachers were yet to come in secretly. The Church, he said, would be infiltrated by heresies. Do you not see this prophecy fulfilled today? Has the Church not been secretly invaded by heretic doctrines? How many times have you heard these false teachers teach that you should believe in them? They tactfully de-emphasize Christ and emphasize themselves.

2Chronicles 20:20, says that you should believe *in* the Lord your God but believe His prophet. It did not say that we should believe *in* His prophet.

> ***Believe in the Lord God, and you shall be established; believe His Prophet,***

and you shall prosper.
2Chron. 20:20

To believe the prophet of God means believing that the words of his prophecy are true and come from God. It actually means believing God. But if you believe *in* His Prophet, that prophet can disappoint you, being still human. So it is falsehood and not Christianity to teach believers to believe in a man. One of such teachers once said that Jesus was imperfect because of Heb. 5:8.

Heresies! They are actually denying the Lord who bought them. Although the Bible clearly teachers that Jesus knew no sin, they prefer to believe lies as heresies instead, provoking God, 2Cor. 5:21

Read the next verse of that misinterpreted text, Heb. 5:9. God perfected Jesus and made Him the author of eternal salvation to all who obey Him. God perfected Him! Paul here was talking about the one hundred percent humanity of Christ. The Lord was one hundred percent man and one hundred percent God. That is part of the mystery of godliness, 1 Tim 3:16

And many will follow their destructive ways, 2Peter 2:2

This is obviously the case today. These false teachers are drawing multitudes to their New Age psychedelic Churches. Many today are following their destructive ways.

…because of whom the way of truth will be blasphemed,
2Peter 2:2

Christianity has suffered greatly in the hands of false teachers. They now justify such sins as masturbation in contradiction of the pure word of our Lord Jesus Christ who reveals that sexual immorality includes mere heart acceptance of the very thought of the act, even without yet committing the act, Matt. 5:27-28. These forget that the works of the flesh that lead to hell and exclusion from God's Kingdom inheritance include lasciviousness, Gal. 5:19. The Web definition of lasciviousness includes prurience, feeling morbid sexual desire or propensity to lewdness. It is the ***feeling*** that the Bible condemns in this passage. Masturbation begins with the feeling or desire for inordinate sex.

Other Web definitions of lasciviousness are 1. Given to or expressing lust: lecherous. 2. Exciting sexual desire: salacious. WorldNet 3.0 Farlex clipart collection (2003-2012) defines lasciviousness as carnality, lubricity, prurience, amativeness, sexiness, amorousness, eroticism, and erotism – the arousal of feeling of sexual desire. Is masturbation not ***the arousal*** as defined? Lubricity, which is the second definition of lasciviousness above, is defined in the book Ologies & -Isms (2008) published by the Gale Group Inc. as "the state or condition of having smooth surface, as to facilitate movement against another surface with a minimum friction." If this does not process-define masturbation, what then does?

Unbelievers no longer have the proper motivations to repent. When they see the way of life of these false teachers and their numerous followers, they conclude that Church is just another business, and not the assembly for eternal life. How terrible this is to the world at large. The devil has done great havoc. We must rise up and challenge the devil by dismantling these heresies, exposing their proponents and sacking these false teachers from our Churches. If they are the leaders in the Churches and they refuse to be sacked, then let us leave their false Churches to them and once more seek the old path, the way of truth that we may not perish with them.

The coming of the Lord is imminent. This is a time to awake out of spiritual slumber and straighten the crooked things in our lives, Rom. 13:11-14.

By covetousness they will exploit you with deceptive words, 2Peter 2:3.

How true the prophecy of the word of God turns out to be. By covetousness they have exploited many people. They have used deceptive words to make multitudes finance their greed. To them, it does not matter how the money is made. Provided you are willing to bring it to them, they will welcome you and even make you a deacon or an elder in their Church. How many Church elders and deacons today are drug dealers, conmen or lawless men of one kind or another? It is because of such practices that the Church of

Jesus Christ is blasphemed. The sinner of course should come to Church to be saved. But there is no excuse that can justify the ordination of an unbeliever to the spiritually exalted office of a deacon (the likes of Philip and Stephen of old?). The Bible has the qualifications for these positions clearly laid down in 1Tim. 3:1-13 and Acts 6:3.

I believe that many of these false teachers really know that the master whose purpose they serve is the devil. So they are not afraid of displeasing God. Rather they are like enemy spies sent to infiltrate the opposing camp. Fellow believers, let us challenge these heretics with the written word of God, flush them out, expose and sack them. Challenge them with the unchanging word of God, 1Tim. 6:10-14.

The Church bank account of many of them is not different from their personal bank account. Some even plainly tell you that the Church belongs to them. So, they will promote or demote whomever they please. We must not be concerned with human promotions or demotions at the detriment of eternal life, Matt. 16:26b, 2Peter 2:12-14.

By covetousness they will exploit you with deceptive words, for a long time their judgment has not been idle, and their destruction does not slumber. 2Peter 2:3

Surely, their judgment is coming. They will utterly perish right in their corruption. Watch them, they go from bad to worse until they will commit hideous crimes against the ruling authorities of the state in their greed and then you will see them perish in their own corruption. When they are accused in the crimes of their greed, their wages or punishment will come right here on earth, first!

Flashback, you can recall the adulterous eyes of these false teachers. You *cannot* change them. The Bible says that they *cannot* cease from sin. All they are out to do is to beguile unstable souls. This is one of the great dangers of instability in faith. Read the word of God.

Wisdom and knowledge will be the stability of your times… Isaiah 33:6

Without the knowledge of the truth from the Bible and its correct application, they will deceive you. So do not play with them, they have a heart trained in covetous practices. They are very selfish and covetous. By their words they can justify anything, calling good evil and evil good, as they choose. They are cursed with a curse.

> ***Woe to those who call evil good and good evil, who put darkness for light, and light for darkness; who put bitter for sweet, and sweet for bitter,***
> ***Isaiah 5:20.***

They are like oracles in their congregations. It does not matter what the Bible says, they can twist words to suit their covetous intent. Murder, stealing or plain cheating is a minor misdemeanor in their sight. And if they choose to, they can easily justify them openly in the Church of Christ – false teachers!

> ***They have forsaken the right way and gone astray, following the way of Balaam the son of Beor who loved the wages of unrighteousness.***

2Peter 2:15

These disciples of Balaam have forsaken Jesus and gone astray. The sooner we realize that their problem is the love of money the better for the Church. They are clouds without rain, Jude 12-13.

There is no remedy for them. When they realize that the power of God is gone, they go to the occult to receive power to push people down in the Church. The lame will be there, but they cannot heal them. The blind will go home without sight. But their own demonstration of God's anointing power is to push down the unstable and faithless, innocent, naïve souls that have come seeking to worship God.

When they hear them speak great swelling words, those who have actually escaped from sin are lured back into error. Although they promise you Christian liberty, they themselves are slaves of sin and corruption.

> ***For when they speak great swelling words of emptiness, they allure through the lust of the flesh, through***

licentiousness, the ones who have actually escaped from those who live in error. While they promise them liberty they themselves are slaves of corruption; for by whom a person is overcome by him also he is brought into bondage, 2Peter 2:18-19

However, God warns the Church; if you have repented genuinely and you allow these people to lure you back into sin in the name of liberty and you return to those evil things that you had forsaken, like a dog returning to its vomit then it will be worse for you at your later end than at your beginning, 2Peter 2:20-22.

Beware and never you *again* be entangled by any of their yokes of bondage. Stand in your true Christian liberty but never use this liberty as a cloak for vice, Gal. 5:1, 13; 1Peter 2:16.

The Bible has all the answers. We are not wrestling against flesh and blood but against diabolical spirits, Eph. 6:12.

These spirits have devised some very effective strategies with which they have attacked the Church, but the Church is under delusion. The strategy on a broad base can be described as INFILTRATION. It is the purpose of God to use this book to expose and highlight some of these strategies of the devil in this end time. This is to re-awaken the Church of Jesus Christ to the truth as set down in the Bible, in preparation for the return of the Lord.

Now, I warn you that many of the deceptions you will find exposed in this book may be common practices in your own Church especially if you are Pentecostal. This book is not an attack on present day Pentecostalism for I myself am a Pentecostal. But this book is a timely rebuke, a chastening and a correction of a loving Father to His dearly beloved children – the Body of Christ, Rev. 3: 19, Prov. 3:11-12, Heb. 12:7-8

The book itself is based on God's illuminations to me. You will find that every illumination set down here is backed completely by Scriptures.

> ***To the law and to the testimony! If they do not speak according to this word, it is because there is no light in them.***
> ***Isaiah 8:20***

I end this preamble with this challenge: If you do not believe these words, can you dispute them scripturally as not being the truth of God's word? I tell you, no man can, for He never changes and His words are forever settled in heaven, Mal. 3:6a; Heb. 13:8; Psalm 119:89.

Bishop Ukaegbu Ogwo

CHAPTER ONE

SPEAKING IN TONGUES

One of the initial signs of receiving the gift of the Holy Spirit or of being baptized in the Holy Spirit is that the recipient speaks in a new tongue, Mark 16:17, Acts 2:4, Acts 10:45-46.

However, it must be noted that speaking in a new tongue (i.e. in a new language) is a sign in this instance. The new tongue, in this case is not the power source. According to Acts 2:4, you are first filled with the Holy Spirit, then you begin to speak in this new language as the

Spirit who has already filled you gives you utterance.

It is dishonesty and hypocrisy to speak as you give yourself utterance. In a true case of baptism in the Holy Spirit by the Lord Jesus Christ, utterance in a new tongue comes supernaturally and it wells up from the inside, from the belly, flowing without any deliberations or thoughts of what to say next. The heart is thrilled beyond measure and the one baptized comes alive as God enters into him according to the promise of our Lord, John 14: 15-18. This event marks the beginning of a new dimension in the believer's spiritual life. Power comes with it, Acts 1:8

When one is truly baptized by Christ, his zeal to preach the gospel is overwhelming. This is one sure test of whether the tongue is of the devil, psychedelic or of God. The tongue we hear today can be broadly classified into these three categories.

Devilish Tongues

The demons can possess a man and by diabolical powers, that man can speak in a language he has never learnt. You could hear a demon possessed erstwhile illiterate Nigerian speaking Polish when he has never crossed the shores of his native country nor ever had the opportunity of associating with Poles to learn their tongue. This is a demonic manifestation of speaking in tongues. Do you wonder that devils also manifest this power? It is only love that the devil has not counterfeited. No wonder the magicians of Egypt also turned their own rods to snakes, as Moses did, before Pharaoh. Sometimes these demonic tongues manifest even in the Church.

Psychedelic Tongue

Another type of tongue speaking is that of following after the example of others. Imitations! Some people, after hearing their pastors and leaders speak, ***"Orobo-robo shantaya,"*** will pick this up and begin to intone the same thing. Before long they are convinced that they are now baptized in the Holy Spirit. They speak as men give them utterance instead of as the Holy Spirit gives them utterance – Acts 2:4. You recognize this group because they always speak the same way their leader speaks. Also their tongues are always the same irrespective of the varied interpretations they give to the tongues at different times. I call this group the Psychedelic tongue group. These are sometimes very well intended but naive and misled believers. They are saved by faith, born again, but not yet baptized in the Holy Spirit although they pretended to be and sometimes even believe that they are. It is part of the devil's ploy to use this means to halt their spiritual progress.

You see, one of the pre-requisites to being baptized in the Holy Spirit is genuine desire and persistent prayer – Luke 11: 9-13. You must ask, seek and knock and then the Father will give you the Holy Spirit, Luke 11:13.

Therefore when the devil has tricked you into believing that you have received already, when truly you have not yet, you will stop praying for this baptism. Thus it will elude you and consequently your Christian life will become stale, routine, uneventful and powerless. Soon, the Church deteriorates into a mere- social club to you. Multitudes of Christians are in this category. Jesus said we should tarry until we are endued with the power of the Holy

Spirit.

> *Behold, I send the promise of My Father upon you; but tarry in the city of Jerusalem until you are endued with power from on high," Luke 24:49.*

To tarry means to wait. The problem with many Christians is that they are in a hurry to achieve. Therefore they set out to do it by self-will and human ability and subsequently fail woefully. You cannot do God's work by human power. It is a spiritual work and needs the enabling of the Holy Spirit, Isaiah 28:16.

If Jesus needed the enabling of the Holy Spirit before launching out into His God-ordained ministry, we need Him even more, Luke 4:18.

> *Then Jesus when He had been baptized came up immediately from the water; and behold, He saw the Spirit of God descending like a dove and alighting upon Him, Matt. 3:16.*

Holy Spirit Tongues

Once you have been born again, you need to do as the disciples of old did – tarry in your Jerusalem. Wait prayerfully for God to fill you with the Holy Spirit power in a baptismal measure. Surely, when the true baptism comes, utterance in the heavenly language will accompany it. The power and supernatural boldness will not be missing. Zeal for evangelism will also be overwhelming. The devil has robbed these psychedelic tongue rappers. Although they are born again, they are totally powerless. A man who has God dwelling in Him has unlimited power at his disposal. One way of finding out whether or not you are in this group is to ask yourself whether you have truly possessed the power of God in you since you began speaking in tongues.

Jesus promised that you shall receive power when the Holy Spirit has come upon you, Acts 1:8. Also you are to wait until you are endued with power from on high, Luke 24:49. The power received through the Holy Spirit baptism is for witnessing for Christ, Acts 1:8. You will find that those who are truly baptized in the Holy Spirit are motivated by the same

Spirit to preach the gospel wherever they are. They bear witness, through the miracles, signs and wonders that follows them, that Jesus is alive today.

> ***You are the light of the world. A city that is set on a hill cannot be hidden, Matt. 5:14.***

If you are speaking in tongues but hardly have any time for evangelism, you may not be speaking by the power of the Holy Spirit. You do not pretend about this. When the Holy Spirit is in you, He will use you as an instrument for His work. Remember that you did not choose Him but He chose you, John 15:16.

Even when you are an old believer, as long as the Holy Spirit is in you, you must be busy doing God's work, preaching the gospel to save lost souls. No pastor is too old for personal evangelism. The Spirit will not let up. He has commanded us to be occupied doing His business now and until the very hour of His return to rapture the saints, Luke 19:13.

This call is even stronger to those who are

ministers, servants of God. When a pastor does not have personal converts, something surely is wrong. When the man of God has become covetous, he will no longer feel the God-given passion for souls. It is only the true Shepherd that can feel the loss of perishing sheep. Hirelings are only after their pay. The covetous pastor has no time for the souls of those who are materially poor. He would rather spend all his visitation hours with those that propose better prospects of material gain to him when converted. Beloved, go for the souls of unbelievers whether poor or rich! God knows how to provide your needs, James 2:1-9.

The third category of tongues in the Church is from he who is truly baptized in the Holy Spirit by the Lord Jesus Christ. He speaks those spirit-stirring, gooseflesh-forming, heavenly languages – as the Holy Spirit gives him utterance. Even if no one understands him, he speaks mysteries to God. His heart is trilled with joy at his appreciation of the multifaceted glory of God's works and deeds. The flow of this heavenly language brings a spiritual energy rather than exhaustion to him. As he speaks, his heart is filled with a peace and an assurance that is not of this planet. He is like a fully re-charged battery ready for use in evangelism. His Christian life is Holy Spirit-motivated. You have no need to urge him on in the work of God. His life is centered on God's word. By the Holy Spirit he is always witnessing for Christ at home, at work, on the street, in taxis and buses, wherever you may find him. His very life is a witness of eternal life. Always, he gives the glory to God and never to himself. You know these people in your own Churches. They may not be pastors or Church leaders in any category but they carry on the gospel work as their Father's work, without requiring human motivation or praise.

They give for the furtherance of the gospel and never expect anything in return from man. When you praise their efforts, they get embarrassed because they are motivated from the inside by the Holy Spirit Himself. They really cannot help doing what they do; they say in their hearts "we are unprofitable servants. We have done what was our duty to do," Luke 17:10.

The former two groups are not like this. The demonic will manifest evil and sin of such a terrible nature that eventually everyone will begin to doubt their genuineness. No doubt they are also powerful. But their power is of the negative kind. Jesus' power is the only means of overcoming them. They even prophesy accurately but always of doom. These people are dangerous to the unsaved because they can initiate them, into their diabolical influences. Prophets of doom! Their lot is in the lake of fire, ultimately!

As for the psychedelic group, they are totally harmless and also powerless. All their Holy Spirit manifestations end as they stop "rapping in tongue." Thereafter, they are even too exhausted to do anything else but slump down to rest from the hectic exercise of speaking in tongues. These are harmless, deceived clowns in spiritual pretense.

The truly baptized not only speak in tongues by the power of the Holy Spirit, they also burn with the zeal for evangelism. They prophesy truth as led by the Holy Spirit. Genuine praise and worship fill their mouths and hearts. If you are saved, you will have a natural affinity towards them because you have the same Spirit of Christ operating in you too even when you are not yet baptized yourself. The love you feel for them is an indication that you are a real child of God, 1John 3:10.

The Gift of Variety of Tongues – 1Cor. 12:28

After the baptism in the Holy Spirit during which the believer first manifested an ability to speak in a new tongue, he may find this phenomenon repeating periodically in his prayers. Here knowledge and honesty are essential. It would be totally dishonest for the believer to pretend that he cannot control the new phenomenon. The blessed and gentle Holy Spirit does not take over your personality by carrying you off into a realm where you cannot stop or control your tongues. You are still a free moral agent with your own volition.

> *And the spirits of the prophets are subject to the prophets. For God is not the author of confusion but of peace, as in all the Churches of the saints, 1Cor. 14:32-33.*

Also the knowledge of the word of God will

teach you to obey that inner urging of the Holy Spirit not to speak in a disorderly manner. Sometimes too a different kind of gift may manifest. It could be the word of wisdom, the word of knowledge, extra-ordinary faith, the gift of healing, the special ability to work miracles, the gift of prophecy, divine ability to discern various kinds of spirit etc.

However the baptized believer may find that thereafter he now possesses a special ability to speak in a variety of languages, 1Cor. 12:14-31. By this gift, God uses the believer thus blessed to pass messages to the Church. This is different from the sign of speaking in tongues manifested at the Holy Spirit baptism in which the one baptized is offering praises and worship to God in an unknown tongue. Here God is using man as His instrument to send messages, instructions, prophecies and edifications to the Church. An interpretation is required for this gift to benefit the Church for which it is meant.

We must realize that all these spiritual gifts are given to the individual believers that each one may use it for the profit of the entire Church,

> *But the manifestation of the Spirit is given to each one for the profit of all… 1 Cor. 12:7.*

It is sinful to use spiritual gifts selfishly. The Holy Spirit distributed them to us all according to His will.

> *But one and the same Spirit works all these things distributing to each individually as He wills, 1Cor. 12:11*

Therefore arrogating the power that comes as a result the manifestation of these spiritual gifts to us is the height of spiritual stupidity. The power is a *gift* meant for the service of others. And it must always be seen as such. Different believers have different kinds of works apportioned to them in the Church by the Holy Spirit. As a result He has also sent forth the different gifts necessary for the performance of these varied tasks. Therefore, although every believer who has been baptized in the Holy Spirit received the baptism with the sign of speaking in tongues, it is not every believer who has received the gift of speaking in a variety of tongues, 1Cor. 12:28-30

The Holy Spirit clearly asks us through Paul the apostle…Do all speak with tongue? 1Cor. 12:13.

> *…All do not speak with tongue, do they? 1Cor. 12:30 (NASB)*

The answer of course is No! It is because here the Holy Spirit is not talking about speaking in tongue as a sign of the Holy Spirit baptism. That one is the only authentic sign given by God to show that one is baptized with the Holy Spirit.

> *While Peter was still speaking these words, the Holy Spirit fell upon all those who heard the word. And those of the circumcision who believed were astonished, as many as came with Peter, because the gift of the Holy Spirit had been poured out on the Gentiles also. For they heard them speak with tongues and magnify God.*
>
> *Then Peter answered, "Can anyone forbid water, that these should not be*

baptized who have received the Holy Spirit just as we have?" Acts 10:44-48

But here the Spirit is referring to speaking in a variety of tongue. Of course not all have this gift. Just as not all are apostles, not all are prophets and not all are teachers, so all do not speak in a variety of tongues. Although most believers who are baptized in the Holy Spirit can manifest all these various gifts in small measures and their own special gifts in extraordinary measures, so believers who are thus baptized in the Holy Spirit can all speak in tongues but only those with the gift of speaking in a variety of tongues can use this gift in a special expanded dimension as will qualify it as their ministry gift.

But there are some whose special gift is speaking in a variety of tongue. These are the special people whom God uses in an orderly manner to speak mysteries to the Church. Their gift however has a limitation of usage in the Church since they cannot be useful to the Church without interpretation.

Although Paul said "I wish you all spoke with tongues but even more that you prophesied,"

(1Cor. 14:5), yet not all can prophecy and similarly not all can speak in tongue. If you do not possess the gift of speaking in a variety of tongue, it does not mean that you are no longer with your gift of the Holy Spirit. The Holy Spirit could in your own case be manifesting in any of the variety of ways I have already mentioned. Relax! The gift of speaking in tongue is even given as the lowest category of the gifts manifestations by the Holy Spirit, 1Cor. 12:28. There are other appointments and gifts that are greater than that of speaking in tongue, 1Cor. 14:5.

The Need for Interpretation

Speaking in tongues is usually for personal edifications, Jude 1:20.

> ***He who speaks in tongue edifies himself but he who prophesies edifies the Church, 1Cor. 14:2***

However, the mysteries that the gifted one speaks could be made to benefit the Church if he possesses the gift of interpretations also. That way those things he speaks in an unknown language could be interpreted for the whole Church to hear and be edified also, 1Cor. 14:5.

Without the gift of interpretation accompanying the gift of tongues or without an available interpreter, the gift of tongues becomes limited in its usefulness. Its usefulness is only limited to the personal edification of the speaker. This is the reason why it ranks lowest in the rung of spiritual gifts.

The purpose of the Holy Spirit in manifesting various spiritual gifts is that each gift should be used for the benefit of the whole Church, 1 Cor. 12:7. This purpose is not achieved in the gift of tongues unless there is interpretation. Therefore whoever has the gift of speaking in a variety of tongues should earnestly pray for the gift of interpretation. This comes simply by praying in faith. Interpretation is an essential part of his spiritual fulfillment. The Lord had promised that by asking, seeking and knocking persistently, He would give us the gifts of the Holy Spirit that we ask of Him.

Therefore whoever has the gift of speaking in a variety of tongues should earnestly pray for the gift of interpretation, Luke 11:9-13.

Apostle Paul counsels us that our zeal for spiritual gifts is that each gift should be used for the benefit of the whole Church, 1Cor. 14:12-13.

Tongues are languages with significance and meaning, 1Cor. 14:10-11. Do not imagine that your psychedelic babblings are now tongues just because nobody understands you. If you are genuine, someone with the gift of interpretation ought to understand your tongue perfectly well and interpret it. By the Holy Spirit, you are rather to be speaking a language that can be interpreted so that the Church may receive the message that God is sending through you to edify His people.

Orderliness in the Church

Although we are not to forbid people from speaking in tongues, yet in the Church, orderliness must reign. The Holy Spirit has a character. He could be grieved or even quenched by behavior that is indecent and disorderly, Isaiah 63:10; Eph. 4:30; I Thess. 5:19.

> ***Therefore, brethren, desire earnestly to prophesy and do not forbid to speak with tongues. Let all things be done decently and in order.***
> ***1Cor. 14:39-40***

This gift of speaking in tongues was abundantly manifested in Paul the apostle, yet in the Church he hardly showed this gift.

> ***I thank God I speak in tongues more than you all yet in the Church I would rather speak five words with my understanding, that I may teach others also, than ten thousand words in a tongue, 1Cor. 14:18-19.***

The gathering of believers is a sacred assembly. God is present wherever we gather, Matt. 18:20. Therefore there must be order in the Church. Confusion must not be seen in our sacred assemblies. Imagine a prayer meeting or night vigil in which all who are present are praying in tongues. A new convert or an unbeliever in that gathering will think that they have all gone crazy.

> ***Therefore if the whole Church comes together in one place, and all speak with tongues, and there comes in those who are uninformed or unbelievers, will they not say that you are out of your mind? 1Cor. 14:23.***

Paul talked about this long ago but in our Churches today, it is a common sight. Sometimes in our prayer meetings, a call is made for believers to pray in tongues. The question now is, is it as the Spirit or as the prayer leader gives you utterance? How can you genuinely speak in an unknown tongue by the power of the Holy Spirit at the instance of a human being? Who then is the motivator, the Holy Spirit or man? Can man dictate to the Holy Spirit what time to declare His mysteries? Does God no longer have the prerogative of time? Acts 1:7.

God expects us to show faith. But we have gone into all kinds of gimmicks in order to find a substitute for faith. God is a searcher of the hearts of men. We cannot deceive Him,

Jer. 17: 9-10. Those who mislead the Church are blind guides. Do not be blind like them. The Lord will root out all their false doctrines with which they have led many astray, Matt. 15:13-14

If you want to fall into a ditch with them, then continue to let them lead you after you have read this book. But if you desire to be saved from the ditch, come out from among them. Follow the word of God, which is a lamp unto our feet, and stop following man, Psalm 119:105. Read the book of Isaiah Chapter 31 and understand the foolishness of trusting in a man that is drawing multitudes rather than trusting in the unchangeable word of God. The devil has infiltrated the Church of Jesus Christ with strange doctrines and practices.

> *Now the Spirit expressly says that in the latter times some will depart from the truth, giving heed to deceiving spirits and doctrines of demons.*
> *1Tim. 4:1*

> *The time has come that people no longer endure sound doctrines but according to their own desires, because*

> ***they have itching ears, they are heaping up for themselves all kinds of teachings. They are turning their ears away from the truth and turning aside to fables, 2Tim. 4:3-4.***

Fables, myths, cock and bull stories – these are most of what we hear these days in place of the gospel message. These days we hear imaginative testimonies of bull-horned demons and mermaids with human bodies and fish tails. Some have even written some fast selling books based on their experiences and encounters with these spirits. These feed the gullibility of ignorant believers. Thank God for the Bible that says that if they speak not according to this word of God, it is because there is no light in them, Isaiah 8:20. Where in the Bible do you find the basis for a belief in some half human and half fish creatures? The faith of many has been eroded by these fantastic stories that only have the effect of magnifying the devil, which was defeated at Calvary.

The Bible says that we are sitting together with Jesus Christ, **far** above all principalities and powers. Also at the name of Jesus every knee bows, whether of things in heaven, on earth or even beneath the earth. Why then should we behave like those who are afraid of demons? I tell you, whatever picture you may paint of Satan and his demons, they remain defeated foes to those who believe. We have the **Lion of the tribe of Judah** inside of us and we have overcome them because greater is He that is in us than he that is in the world. If the devil can succeed in creating **fear, doubt or unbelief** in you, then and then only can he get you. But if you know your right through the word of God, you will not allow false doctrines to have entrance into your spirit-man.

The instructions are clearly set down in the Bible that, in the church,

> *If anyone speaks in a tongue, let there be two or at the most three, each in turn, and let one interpret. But if there is no interpreter, let him keep silent in church, and let him speak to himself and God, 1Cor. 14:27-28*

But today the prayer times in churches, especially in the Pentecostal circles, is simply a bedlam. Every believer tries to speak in tongues louder than his brother. Just sit back and think of the church of 1Corinthians 14:27-28. I see a most orderly and reverent church in which the gentle character of the Holy Spirit is truly manifested, 1Cor. 14:33.

So you cannot claim that this is not the tradition of your own church. The Bible says **"as in all the churches of the saints."** Matt.15:3, 6, 15:9, Luke 16:15.

Foreigners may do it but that does not make it right! One day God will bring these works to test. They shall be tested by fire and surely suffer loss of reward. Our standards should not be judged by the opinion of the majority but rather by the express word of God. Christian liberty does not mean disobedience to God's word. God hates lawlessness.

> *Whoever commits sin also commits Lawlessness and sin is lawlessness, 1John 3:4, Matt. 7:23*

Even though we are not under the law now that grace has come, yet it is **the law of sin and death** that we are not under. We are, so to speak, under a different kind of law called **the law of the Spirit of life in Christ Jesus**

For the law of the Spirit of life in Christ Jesus has made me free from the law of sin and death, Rom. 8:2.

The law of the **Spirit of life in Christ makes us to observe all the righteous requirements of the law of sin and death**. There is something that the law was trying to teach us. But now that faith has come we are no longer under a teacher. However, we are not to discard his lessons but to apply the righteousness taught us by the law in the liberty and freedom by which Christ has made us free.

> *but before faith came, we were kept under guard by the law, kept for the faith which would after-wards be revealed. Therefore the law was our tutor to bring us to Christ, that we might be justified by faith. But after faith has come, we are no longer under a tutor, Gal. 3:23-25*
>
> *For you brethren, have been called to*

liberty; only do not use liberty as an opportunity for the flesh, but through love serve one another, Gal. 5:13

If God is not the author of the confusion and bedlam we see in the churches today, who then is? Of course it is the devil that has infiltrated the church. The custodians of the word, the ministers of the gospel are too busy chasing material gains to speak the truth to the blind and wandering flock of Jesus Christ. But thank God for the corrections of today. If after reading these words, you leave your flock without implementing these corrections, you will have no one else to blame but yourself. When he that called you will ask you to give Him an account of your stewardship, you can never claim ignorance. The word of God is there for you to see for yourself, Luke 16:1-2. God is not the author of confusion *but of peace*. Is the Prince of peace in your church, Isaiah 9:6? When the Prince of Peace reigns in your church, His gifts will not cause you to be sweating. Rather you will relax in the bliss of the days of heaven upon this earth, Deut. 11:21.

The fact that you are a victim of this deception

does not make you any less a child of God rather you are a child that has been deceived. All you need to do is to confess and forsake the path of deception and God will restore you and then real growth will commence in your spiritual life. However, there is still more to come. As He unfolds our errors, let us not harden our hearts choosing to maintain church traditions. Rather let us observe to do according to all that is contained in the Bible (Josh.1:8), not turning to the right hand or to the left in order to amend or modify the word of God to suit present trends, Deut. 28:14. It is only then that you will make your ways prosperous and have good success.

Groaning which cannot be Uttered-Rom. 8:26

It is typical of the devil to take a Scripture and, quoting it out of context, deceive men into misapplying it. He did it with Eve and succeeded but when he tried it with our Lord Jesus Christ, Satan failed woefully, Gen.3:1-7 cf. Luke 4:1-12. When God revealed that in making intercession for us, the Holy Spirit does this with groaning, it was clearly stated that those groaning *couldn't* be uttered. Today

Satan has introduced animal and demonic noises in the prayer of the saints. Imagine the Holy Communication between the Redeemed of the Lord and the Most High Himself being an object of demonic influence. So instead of offering quality prayers, the believer wastes valuable hours making unintelligible noises all in the name of groaning in the spirit. We have been deceived!

The powerful prayers and singing of Paul and Silas shook prison foundations threw open the prison doors and broke the chains and shackles that held them bound. The Bible says that as they were praying and singing the prisoners were listening to them, Acts 16:25-26

This means that those powerful and effective prayers were not in tongues. When the early Church was persecuted, they prayed in boldness, raising their voice to God "in one accord" (in an orderly manner without confusion) and said:

> ***Lord you are God…Now, Lord, look on their threats, and grant to your servants that with all boldness they may speak your word…***

Acts 4:24-30

Among these believers were those that experienced Pentecost, the beginning of this outpouring of the Holy Spirit with the sign of speaking in tongues, yet in this their hour of distress and pressure, they prayed a united prayer in understanding (rather than in tongues). If you pray corporate prayer in tongues, how would the others who do not understand your tongue know when to say Amen? 1Cor. 14:7-12, 16-19.

He who speak in a tongue edifies himself, but he who prophesies edifies the Church, 1Cor. 14:4

Tongues are for private closet prayers. Whenever prayers involve more than one person praying together, it is unedifying to pray in tongues. ***Unless there is available interpretation, prayers in tongues should not be made in the church.*** Paul and Silas had to pray in understanding because they were two. The early apostolic Church also expressed their request in a clear common language and what was the result? Their place of gathering was shaken and they were filled with the Holy

Spirit which made them able to move out and evangelize in boldness, Acts 4:31. In other words, they received answers to their prayers.

The devil came to the Church and introduced groaning and now true believers are deceived into making animal noises rather than praying. I believe that some church leaders today have gone to the occult to obtain power. So Satan uses them to bring in strange teachings and heresies to deceive many. Beware! Do not let any man be your standard but, rather, let your standard be the word of God that never changes.

Those groaning or noises are demonic. When the Lord Jesus Christ was faced with the task of going to the cross and He was in agony, we have our perfect example of prayers in times of distress. Even though His soul was exceedingly sorrowful even to death, we were not told that He groaned in animal noises. If He did, He would have woken up his disciples who were fast asleep. Matt. 26:27-47:Mark 14: 33-42: Luke22:39-46.

> ***And being in agony, He prayed more earnestly. And His sweat became like***

> ***great drops of blood falling down to the ground, Luke 22:44.***

The believer should pray more earnestly rather than make animal noises.

> ***The effective fervent prayer of a righteous man avails much,***
> ***James 5:16***

Earnest prayer has nothing to do with bodily exercise or movements. Earnestness refers to the depth of spiritual impact the prayer makes upon the one praying. It means praying with seriousness, fervency and determination. It makes prayer a serious business and not a light- hearted affair. The one praying earnestly is the one who has determined to receive an answer before he rises. It reflects the level of commitment of the believer to seeing his prayer answered.

Brethren, let us come out of deception and go back to the old path. There is no substitute to faith. If you do not have faith in what God has promised to do for you, no amount of groaning in animal noises can make God substitute noise for faith.

But without faith it is impossible to please Him…Heb. 11:6

Rather than groan and bodily- labor in your prayers like the prophets of Baal before Elijah, simply believe in the name of Jesus and pray according to the simplicity of His gospel. He will surely come to your aid. It is faith that moves His hand, not emotions. All those noises can only make you to lose your voice. They cannot cause any prayers to be answered. Be wise and do not be deceived. As you read these words, take positive action in putting a stop to all these unscriptural practices. As you do His will, His blessings shall be mightily released in your life in Jesus name.

These false doctrines are the unrighteous deceptions spoken of in 2 Thess. 2:9-12. God will send a strong delusion to those who refuse the truth so that they will believe a lie. Today many do not believe the truth but are rather pleased in doing whatever is unrighteous. I pray that if you are affected, the Lord will deliver you from this deception that you may be re-awakened to the truth of His word.

CHAPTER TWO

"SLAIN" UNDER ANOINTING

It is surprising how Christians can so easily be deceived, how gullible believers are. It is as if to say that since they are **believers** then they can believe anything. God does not expect believers to believe just any doctrine but the written word of God. Any doctrine that has no stand and root in the Bible is not of God.

To the law and to the testimony! If they do not speak according to this word, it

> *is because there is no light in them.*
> *Isaiah 8:20*

Even then, the doctrine must be supported by at least two or three separate instances in the Bible. For out of the mouth of two or three witnesses shall every word be established, Deut. 19:15; Matt. 18:16

Jesus Example John 18:4-8

Unfortunately today, false teachers lift passages in the Bible arbitrarily and weave their demonic doctrines around them. A good example is the event at Gethsemane recorded by the apostle John.

> *Jesus therefore, knowing all things that would come upon Him, went forward and said to them, 'Whom are you seeking?' They answered Him, 'Jesus of Nazareth.' Jesus said to them, 'I am He.' And Judas who betrayed Him also stood with them. Then when He said to them 'I am He,' they drew back and fell to the ground, John 18: 4-6*

After the three hours of powerful, mountain-moving prayers of our Lord Jesus Christ, he confronted men and the power of anointing that He exuded as a result of having been with the Father, pushed them to the ground. Today the doctrine of being *"slain" under anointing* has become over-abused in the Pentecostal circles. I once attended a prayer meeting during which people were encouraged to fall in demonstration that they had received answers to their prayers.

Reason for Falling

When a man has been before the presence of God and received special anointing, men may not easily stand before him. When Moses went before God, the glory of the Lord rubbed off on him and the skin of his face shone such that Israel was afraid to come near him, Exodus 34:29-35. This was the kind of power that was manifest in a greater dimension upon the Lord Jesus at the garden of Gethsemane. Today this power still manifests when men spend quality prayer time with the Lord. They emerge filled with power and lesser mortals may not stand their presence but would bow to the Spirit of God in them. This is how people could be "slain" under the anointing. Sometimes this power is manifest at the physical contact with the anointed one. At other times the anointed may be totally unaware of the effect he is having on others. However this is a healthy manifestation of the power of the Holy Spirit. I have personally been taken unawares by this manifestation. Without the least intention to demonstrate God's power thus, I laid hand on someone to pray for her and the next thing I knew, she was flat on the floor.

When the Holy Spirit wants to manifest Himself in this way He will. You are not to go around persuading people to fall on the ground or be disappointed if they do not fall. The power of the Holy Spirit must not be arrogated to man. So why do you bother that people are not pushed down in your services?

When the anointing is present, the entire congregation could bow at the power of God's anointed one. But it is vain to seek for power for the sake of such demonstrations. You should rather ask God to give you power to heal the sick, the blind and the lame - power to raise the dead. These are profitable demonstrations of God's power that have scriptural support and will positively advertise the gospel of our Lord Jesus Christ. This is the type of demonstration of God's power that you should aspire for. Do not forget that the power comes by prayer, the power to do *good works.*

Receiving By Falling

It is totally unscriptural to teach your congregation that it is a sign of having received blessing from God when you are "slain" under anointing. Those who came with clubs and knives to arrest Jesus at Gethsemane certainly did not receive any blessing when they fell to the ground before the Lord. As usual the gullibility of many believers makes them desperate to receive, Phil. 4:6-7,

Some may even go to the extent of imagining themselves pushed down by a supposed anointing. In their desperation to receive, they crash to the ground at the preacher's continuous urging. If you ask them, they are unsure but **"think"** that they fell under anointing.

Of course you always have the pretenders who will fall at the first suggestion that it is the means of receiving blessings from God. Let every man be careful how he uses the name of the Holy Spirit. Do not deceive your flock by persuading them to fall in demonstration that you are a powerful man of God. Our Lord Jesus Christ, who is our example, never did that. Do not help the Holy Spirit but rather let Him have His way. If you have no spiritual strength, go and wait on the Lord, Isaiah 40:31. There is no substitute to prayer. When you give God quality time, He will give you quality anointing and you will even raise the dead in Jesus' name.

The Role of Magic

It is not unknown that preachers, who have lost the anointing of God, like King Saul of old, have gone to the mediums, spiritists or sorcerers to obtain alternative power. The devil will of course give them demonic power with which to perform signs and lying wonders in order to deceive the gullible.

> ***Now the Spirit expressly says that in later times some will depart from the faith, giving heed to deceiving spirits and doctrines of demons, 1Tim. 4:1***

> *The coming of the lawless one is according to the working of Satan, with all power, signs and lying wonders, 2Thess. 2:9*

These people are always in the negative. Their prophecies are almost always of doom. They preach death and hardly talk about life. They tactfully exult the devil in their churches and subtly encourage men to live in perpetual fear of Satan. Their claim to miracles lies only in performance of unprofitable signs. Unprofitable power is what they can demonstrate. These people have specialized in making people fall under their supposed anointing. Many who come to church in order to meet with God inadvertently end up being initiated into their diabolical schemes.

Once a female banker in Lagos told me that she attended one such session and she was "slain" under this demonic anointing. From that moment, she discovered that she could no longer pray to God. Whenever she closed her eyes in prayer, that power would return to push her down. The devil is going to and fro causing spiritual havoc in the lives of many.

Tell me how such a spirit could be of God. Can the Spirit of God Who tells us to pray without ceasing (1Thess.5: 17) prevent one from praying? No wonder we are told not to believe every spirit.

> *Beloved, do not believe every spirit, but test the spirits, whether they are of God; because many false of prophets have gone out into the world,*
> *1Thess. 4:1*
>
> *But examine everything carefully; hold fast to that which is good,*
> *1Thess. 5:21 (NASB)*

Better know it now that there are lying spirits. Magicians are in our Churches today. This is the reality of the situation. Remember that Simon the sorcerer saw people speaking in tongues by the laying on of hands of the apostles and he was thrilled at the prospect of having such a power at his disposal. He even offered to pay for it. Today the magicians and sorcerers have invaded our churches and they are practicing magic in the name of Jesus. Remember that –

> *...If they speak not according to this word (the Bible) it is because there is no light in them, Isaiah 8:20*

The performance of mighty wonders is not a sign of God's approval. God hates lawlessness, Matt. 7:21-23.

The Bible should serve as a lamp to light up our spiritual paths.

> *Your word is a lamp to my feet and a light to my path. Psalm 119:105*

When they introduce a new one, do not be weak. Be bold to ask for the scriptural basis of what they teach. You should believe every word of God and doubt every doctrine that has no root in the Bible. The Bible as a whole is given so that you may be complete and thoroughly equipped.

> *All Scripture is giving by inspiration of God and is profitable for doctrine, for reproof, for correction, for instruction in righteousness that the man of God may be complete, thoroughly equipped*

for every good work, 2Tim. 3:16-17.

There is nothing that needs to be added to the Bible to make you better equipped. Adding things to the Bible brings a curse. Changing the gospel brings a curse. The Bible is complete. Any change to the Bible is a perversion of the gospel of Jesus Christ.

> *I marvel that you are turning away so soon from Him who called you in the grace of Christ to a different gospel which is not another; but there are some who trouble you and want to pervert the gospel of Christ. But even if we, or an angel from heaven preach any other gospel to you than what we have preached to you, let him be accursed. As we have said before, so now I say again, if anyone preaches any other gospel to you than what you have received, let him be accursed,*
> *Gal. 1:6-9*

At the very end of the Bible the following words are written:

For I testify to everyone who hears the word of the prophecy of this book, if anyone adds to these, God will add to him the plagues that are written in this book and if anyone takes away from the words of the book of this prophecy, God will take his part from the Book of life, from the holy city and from the things which are written in this book, Rev 22:18-19.

Two verses after these words, the Bible ends. So these are like the last words of the Holy Scripture. Take heed that you do not reject them. Rather reject all false doctrines and you will be able to stand in Jesus name.

Therefore submit to God. Resist the devil and he will flee from you, James 4:7

Therefore take up the whole armor of God, that you may be able to withstand in the evil day and having done all to stand. Stand therefore, having girded your waist with truth, having put on the breastplate of righteousness, Eph. 6:13-14.

One consolation we have is that the power of these magicians in the churches does not work against real repentant, born again Christians, even when such Christians are at the lowest ebb of their prayer lives. We have a promise of protection from our Father who never lies. We are protected as long as we are living sin-free lives.

> *No weapon formed against you shall prosper... Isaiah 54:17*
>
> *He who dwells in the secret place of the Most High, shall abide under the shadow of the Almighty, Psalms 91:1.*
>
> *For there is no sorcery against Jacob nor is there any divination against Israel, Num. 23:23.*

My brother, my sister, we are covered once we are born again and are living right. As long as Christ is in you, and you do not break your hedge, you are super- protected.

> *For he who touches you touches the apple of His eyes. 'For I,' says the*

> *Lord, 'will be a wall of fire around her, and I will be the glory in her midst,' Zech. 2:5*

> *You are of God, little children, and have overcome them, because He who is in you is greater than he who is in the world, 1John 4:4.*

> *Whatever is born of God does not sin. He that is born of God keeps himself and the wicked one does not touch him, 1John 5:18.*

But do not forget that we are born again by faith and so it is also faith that guarantees our protection. Never allow the devil to persuade you that he can prevail against you. Talk back the Scriptures to him. Dispel fear totally from encroaching into your life. When they persuade you to fall, stand fast in your liberty.

> *It was for freedom that Christ set us free. Therefore keep standing firm and do not be subjected again to a yoke of slavery, Gal. 5:1(NASB).*

Do not allow them to yoke you again into their bondage. You are now above them in Christ Jesus. Refuse to come down from your mountain of faith to their valley of doubt and unbelief. Be patient. God will bring you the answer you seek in due time in Jesus name.

And the desire of the righteous will be granted, Prov. 10:24.

Your answered prayer will elude you if you allow them to make you fall into their demonic antics. Never doubt the power of God and you will soon see His victory manifested for you in Jesus name. If however, you have already fallen victim to their diabolic influence, the cure is repentance. When Jesus comes in, Satan will flee. Where there is light, darkness cannot abide there,

All believers in Christ have authority against the enemy, Luke 10:19. We are all seated together with Christ at the right hand of the throne of majesty. Therefore stop running to and from. By your own faith-filled prayer, this problem will be over. As soon as you are born again, there is anointing that comes upon your life that can destroy demonic yokes. Your own prayer of faith activates this anointing. There is no need to run to and fro seeking help. Yes, the anointing in another Spirit-filled believer can do the trick if he prays in faith for you. But your own God-given anointing can also do the same thing for you, Isaiah 52:1-2, Luke 17:21-22. The anointing of the Holy Spirit (not by particular individuals) solves the problem of the yoke, Isaiah 10:27.

The Character of the Anointed

Anointing is like oil in a vessel. The vessel in this case is the man that is anointed. That is why Paul the apostle wrote to Timothy,

> ***If any man cleanses himself… he will be a vessel for honor, sanctified and useful for the Master, prepared for every good work, 2Tim 2:21.***

You must cleanse yourself from all uncleanness for you to be God's anointed one. How do you do this? By fleeing youthful lust, pursuing righteousness, faith, love and peace with those who call on the Lord out of a pure heart… 2Tim 2:22-26.

> *Be clean you who bear the vessels of the Lord, Isaiah 52:11.*

God expects purity and holiness to be evident in the lives of His anointed ones. When Samson sinned, the Spirit of God left him, even though he did not know it then.

> *And she said, 'The Philistines are upon you, Samson!' So he awoke from his sleep, and said, I will go out as before, at other times, and shake myself free! But he did not know that the LORD had departed from him, Judges 16: 20.*

Many had been anointed but today the Holy Spirit has departed from them because of sin. Thus they blunder on without the power of God backing their ministries. Some of them have fallen into the deadly error of seeking alternative power from Satan instead of repenting and asking God for His restoration. When a preacher lives contrary to the word he preaches then beware of him for he is dangerous. When your pastor goes into self-glory and covetousness then the devil has taken captive of him. Jesus says that you will distinguish the false from the genuine **by their**

fruits, Matt. 7:15-29. That church where the congregation is held in perpetual fear of their spiritual leader is a church in bondage.

> *But Jesus called them to Himself and said to them, 'You know that those who are considered rulers over the gentiles lord it over them and their great ones exercise authority over them.* **Yet it shall not be so among you;** *but whoever desires to become great among you shall be your servant. And whoever of you desires to be first shall be last. For even the Son of Man did not come to be served but to serve, and to give his life a ransom for many,*
> *Mark 10:42-45.*

The real liberty comes in the freedom of loving fearlessly. When the doctrines of a church are made to suit and satisfy the covetous whims of the leader, them beware. You may unintentionally make yourself an idol worshipper, worshipping your church leader under his doctrines instead of worshipping God based on His word.

> *But to the wicked God says: 'What right have you to declare my statutes, or take my covenant in your mouth, seeing you hate instructions and cast my words behind you,' Psalm 50:16-17*

There is no preacher who is above the word that he preaches. When the preacher cannot obey God's word, leave him. He is no longer qualified to lead the people of God; neither can the truth of God continue to flow through him. Sooner than later whatever word he manifests can only be diabolical. Do not be deceived. The simple formula that the Lord gave to us is this:

> *...by their fruits you will know them, Matt. 7:16-20.*

The mouth is an overflow valve of the heart. When the heart is full, its contents will spill over, out of the mouth. A bad heart when full will spill out evil utterances out of the mouth of the owner. A bad heart will produce evil fruits ultimately.

> *Either make the tree good and its fruit good, or else make the tree bad and its*

fruit bad; for a tree is known by its fruit. Brood of vipers, how can you, being evil, speak good things? For out of the abundance of the heart the mouth speaks. A good man, out of the good treasure of his heart brings forth good things, and an evil man out of the evil treasure brings forth evil things, Matt 12:33-35.

Therefore, watch their lives. You will come to know whether they are of God or of the devil. When the preacher begins to claim that it is impossible to live above sin, watch it, he is most likely living in sin at that very moment. Study the word of God in Romans chapter six. Certain truths are clearly portrayed. Any attempts to be righteous by human ability always fail. But if you go by faith, you will discover that, of a truth, the miracle of your new birth and co- death with Christ sets you free from sin. Daily present yourself to God as an instrument of righteousness, as being *alive to God and dead to sin,* then sin will no longer have dominion over you.

Likewise you also reckon yourselves to be dead indeed to sin, but alive to God *in Christ Jesus our Lord. Therefore do not let sin reign in your mortal body, that you should obey, it in its lust. And do not present your members (body parts)* as instruments of unrighteousness to sin, but present yourselves to God as being alive from the dead and your members as instruments of righteousness to God for sin shall not have dominion over you for you are not under law but under grace...*

Do you not know that to whom you present yourselves slaves to obey, you are that one's slaves whom you obey, whether of sin to death or of obedience to righteousness? ...and having been set free from sin, you become slaves of righteousness...

For just as you presented your members as slaves of uncleanness, so now present your members (your body parts)* as slaves of righteousness for holiness. ...But now having been set free from sin, and having become slaves of God, you have your fruit to

> *holiness and the end, everlasting life. Rom. 6:18-19, 22*
- Bracketed words mine

If you do this daily presentation by faith and you always reckon yourself as righteous and dead to sin, you will find that sin will not have dominion over you. You should always be **righteousness conscious.** The reason that God made provision for confession is as a contingency, in order to bring back to the right path those who slip off the path of life. But do not live your life perpetually confessing sins. Live righteous by faith. All things are possible with those who believe, Mark 9:23.

> *My little children, these things I write to you,* **that you may not sin**. *And if anyone sins, we have an advocate with the Father, Jesus Christ the righteous. And He himself is the propitiation for our sin, and not for ours only but also for the whole world, 1John 2:1-2.*

Just because you have a Lawyer in Heaven pleading your case, you do not have to remain in sin. Jesus was not manifested to take away our sins in order to make room for us to commit new ones.

> ***And you know that He was manifested to take away our sins, and in Him there is no sin. Whoever abides in Him does not sin. Whoever sins (remains in sin)* has neither seen Him nor known Him, 1John 3:5-6***

* Bracketed words mine

For you to live above sin, you must abide in Christ. To abide means **to remain or to dwell in Christ.** It involves a perpetual awareness of His presence within you. It does not involve a hit and run kind of relationship. Whoever abides in Him does not sin. If you want the true righteousness that comes from the Lord Jesus Christ, then abide in Him. By faith you can reckon yourself always in His presence. You can see Him always in your joys, sadness, abundance, trials, afflictions, etc. When you live this way, you are truly living by faith, Hab. 2:4.

Those who do not understand this attempt righteousness by their own ability, by works.

They do not *reckon* their righteousness *as* being a manifestation of the character of the Christ within them Therefore they fail woefully. When they have failed, they come back to preach that righteousness is an impossibility. My friend, you are deceived. The only pre-requisite to being raptured is holiness, Eph. 4:25-27.

> *Pursue peace with* **all men** *and* **holiness** *without which no one will see the Lord, Heb. 12:14.*

Therefore when the anointing is no longer evident in the life of a minister who was mightily manifesting the true power of God in the past, watch out, it is a dangerous signal.

> *When you saw a thief, you consented with him and have been a partaker with adulterers you give your mouth to evil and your tongue frames deceit, Psalm 50:18-19.*

These days we hear of pastors that welcome money from every source, supporting even con men in their evil machinations and quoting

Scriptures to justify their acts of deceit. Verse 22 of that passage warns:

> *Consider this you who forget God, lest I tear you to pieces and there is none to deliver.*

God is really angry with you pseudo-pastors. Repent now and return to God. Yes you should welcome sinners of the worst kind to the church but you should not encourage them in their sin. You must continuously condemn evil openly until they repent. Tell them that their ill-gotten money is abhorrent to God and let them feel the dirtiness of their distasteful wealth. When you do this, many of them will repent and the true believer will be proud to be called a believer in Christ. In fact when you preach the truth persistently, there will come a time when they will be too ashamed to flaunt their ill-gotten wealth in the church. The dupes in government will be too ashamed to acquire dubious wealth when they know that they have their pastor and brethren to contend with in the explanation of the source of their sudden wealth The dignity of the church will thus be restored and the clergy held in high honor. Thus God our Father will be glorified through this knowledge and manifestation of the character of our Lord Jesus in Christ in us.

CHAPTER THREE

MISDIRECTED MILITANCY

And from the days of John the Baptist the kingdom of heaven suffers violence and the violent take it by force,
Matt. 11:12

Many have used this passage of the Bible to excuse their expressions of hatred, wrath and unforgiving spirit. How many times have you heard this passage quoted in the church and prayer meetings before the release of curses, venom and even death on the enemies of the saints – both physical and spiritual At other times we hear, ***Suffer not a witch to live.*** And subsequently believers would be urged to use their spiritual daggers and pierced the hearts of their detractors – human and spiritual – in revenge; and also as an expression of the required violence to take the Kingdom of God by force.

Brethren, these things ought not to be so. It is a misapplication of the word of God. In Ephesians chapter 6 verse 12, the Bible clearly tells us that we are not contending or wrestling against flesh and blood but against diabolical **spirits.** Witches and wizards are flesh and blood. Recall that when a Samaritan village rejected our Lord Jesus, His disciples James and John requested that they should command fire to come down from heaven and consume them j***ust as Elijah did.*** But Jesus replied in rebuke:

> ***You do not know what manner of spirit you are of. For the Son of Man did not come to destroy men's lives but to save them, Luke 9:55-56.***

Our violence is against principalities and powers, against the rulers of the darkness of this age, against the spiritual host of wickedness in heavenly places and not against flesh and blood, Eph. 6:12

Jesus came to this world to show us the right path. In the dispensation of Elijah he was justified in his action. But after Jesus came to show us how to do God's will, you cannot operate in that old way and expect God to back you up. Clearly Jesus was telling James and John that they have a different kind of spirit from that of Elijah. As a believer you must come to the recognition of the character of the Spirit of Christ in you and let that character unfold out of you.

The Mount of Transfiguration, Mark 9:2-8

On this mountain, the Lord was transfigured before Peter and the same James and John. Later, Moses and Elijah appeared. Filled with fear, Peter spoke from common sense:

> ***Rabbi, it is good for us to be here, and let us make three tabernacles, one for***

you, one for Moses and one for Elijah, Mark 9:5.

Many ignorant believers are doing just that today. In their hearts they have even more than these three tabernacles. Some who have these varied tabernacles erected in their hearts still burn incense and candles during prayers. They still offer the sacrifices of pigeons, bulls and goats despite the ultimate sacrifice of Christ made once and for all, Heb. 10:5-12

They still insist on wearing the literal white garment despite the Bible explanation that pure linen is the righteous acts of the saints. They perpetually oil their head instead of getting anointed spiritually by the Holy Spirit. This is not to say that applying the anointing oil is wrong but the oil must be reckoned by faith to represent the Holy Spirit anointing in the spirit realm. And anointing oil must be properly ministered by the elders and not by individuals according to the Scriptures, James 5:14.

Let your garments always be white and let your head lack no oil, Eccl. 9:8.

And to her it was granted to be arrayed in fine linen, clean and bright, for the fine linen is the righteous act of the saints, Rev. 19:8.

Now when he had taken the scroll, the four living creatures and the twenty-four elders fell down before the lamb, each having a harp, and golden bowls full of incense, which are the prayers of the saints, Rev. 5:8.

(See also Psalm 141:2; Rev. 8: 3-4.)

In reply to Peter's ignorant suggestion came the voice of God out of the cloud that overshadowed them:

> ***This is My beloved Son; hear Him, Mark 9:7.***

It is interesting to note that at this declaration from the Father, both Moses and Elijah vanished from the sight of their audience.

> *Suddenly, when they had looked around, they saw no one anymore,* **but only** *Jesus with themselves, Mark 9:8.*

You are still looking around today; you will see no one anymore but Jesus. We, who are men on earth today, are to hear only Jesus in this our dispensation. We have been left with **only Jesus.** God here is telling not only James and John but also us today especially. We are to hear Jesus only and no longer Moses the Law and Elijah the Prophet. Therefore the likes of the attitude of Elijah in calling for the death of sinners (of any kind) is to be replaced with the attitude of Christ. Even Moses in his time forewarned Israel of the coming of Jesus whom he commanded them to obey in all things whatsoever He says, Deut. 18:15-19.

> *For Moses truly said to the fathers, the Lord your God will raise up for you a prophet like me from your brethren. Him you shall hear in all things, whatever He says to you, and it shall come to pass that every soul who will not hear that Prophet shall be utterly destroyed from among the people, Act 3:22-23.*

You ought to read the Bible as one single homogeneous book and message and not just lift off passages in isolation. The messengers of Satan are thus using the Bible to justify false doctrines. Follow the trend of the Scriptures and know what God's expectation of you is today. Know the dispensation you are in and how the truth of God is being unfolded over the generations.

Olive Oil Ministration

It is really unfortunate that the Pentecostals of today have delved so far into ignorant occultism that you can hardly tell the difference between them and the spirit cults like the white garment churches. Scripturally, olive oil is to be ministered by the elders of the Church for the healing of the sick in the New Testament.

> *Is anyone among you sick? Let him call for the elders of the church and let them pray over him, anointing him with oil in the names of the Lord; and the prayer offered in faith will restore the one who is sick, and the Lord*

will raise him up and if he has committed sins, they will be forgiven him, James 5:14-15 (NASB).

It is noteworthy that the elders of the church are to minister the oil unto the sick. It is not for the sick people to minister the oil unto themselves. Also it was not the oil that brought the healing but rather the prayer of faith offered after anointing the sick with the oil. But today we find that the oil is used by the sick like medicine to be administered as the need arises.

The Risk of Idolatry

Let me state clearly that a minister can give any instruction to the sick and if he obeys in faith, healing will result. The sick could even be told to jump up seven times and if he believes, he will be healed if he obeys. However in this ministration, care should be taken that one does not inadvertently slip into occultism. By a deliberate will of God, He does not want Christianity or the worship of Jehovah to focus on material things, images and symbols unlike all the other religions.

> *You shall have no other gods before Me. You shall not make for yourself an idol or any likeness of what is in heaven above or on the earth or in the water under the earth,*
> *Exodus 20:3-4 (NASB).*

God wants man to worship Him in spirit.

> *But an hour is coming and now is, when the true worshippers shall worship the Father in Spirit and truth for such people the Father seeks to be His worshippers. God is Spirit and those who worship Him must worship in Spirit and truth,*
> *John 4:23-24(NASB)*

Therefore any focus away from the spiritual unto the materials realm as symbols of Jehovah worship does not have His approval. That was why the brazen serpent had to be destroyed, even though it was God who instructed Moses to erect it for the healing of the children of Israel – it was becoming a form of idolatry.

Then the Lord God said to Moses, 'Make a fiery serpent and set it on a standard and it shall come about, that everyone who is bitten, when he looks at it he shall live,
Numbers 21:8 (NASB).

And he did what was right in the sight of the Lord according to all that his father David had done. He removed the high places and broke down the sacred pillars and cut down the Asherah. He also broke in pieces the bronze serpent that Moses had made, for until those days the sons of Israel burned incense to it, and it was called Nehustan,
2Kings 18:3 (NASB).

This is one area the Roman Catholic Church must address without delay. Mary worship, prayers to dead saints and erection of worshipped images are forms of idolatry. Even in some Protestant churches, the cross is worshipped and bowed to. This is evil and excites the jealousy of Jehovah God, Exodus 20: 5. The glory of God has left the physical altar and is now in the spiritual altar within the believer's heart, 1Cor. 3:16 and 6:19.

In the same way, God resists any attempt to make olive oil another form of idol. Do not join the crowd of those that use olive oil as a talisman. Properly ministered by the elders of the Church, God uses the oil to represent a spiritual work that he does. The Hebrew word ***Shemen*** translated in Isaiah 10:27 to mean **anointing oil** has as one of its several meanings: fatness, of a fat bull which has cast off its yoke and broken loose, Deut.32: 15; Hosea 4:6 Therefore, the anointing oil is symbolic of breaking loose from the yoke of bondage. The power is not in the oil but in the spiritual words of the prayers offered. Do not be confused.

If allowed, Satan can capitalize on this ignorance and build a false doctrine of idolatry around it. This he has already begun to do. Today, we see people who have no places for obedience to God's word, but they are interested in the miracles, signs and wonders that come from God. These are sometimes taught to put some of their anointed olive oil into handkerchiefs and to rub this over their face before proceeding for important business ventures and meetings. Such a practice is to ensure success in these ventures. Sure enough, as they do this success manifests. Occultism in the church! Repent and be delivered from the powers of darkness. Nowhere is such a practice ***scripturally approved or recommended***. Men's hearts are in God's hands to influence to your favor if you are in the will of God, Proverbs 21:1. But such an influence comes only through prayers. It will profit you nothing to gain the whole world and lose your soul.

> *And He summoned the twelve and began to send them out in pairs and He was giving them authority over the unclean spirits...*
>
> *And they went out and preached that men should repent. And they were casting out many demons and were anointing with oil many sick people and healing them,*
> *Mark 6:7, 12-13 (NASB).*

It was the Lord Jesus Himself who summoned His apostles out of the multitude of disciples that He had. Even then, He still sent them out in pairs. This once again demonstrates that olive oil ministration is an elder's ministration, not a one man's affair. Notice also that these apostles first preached repentance from sin before the ministration of deliverance and healing.

But men have today specialized in deliverance without salvation from sin. A genuine concern for the perishing souls will not allow the minister to have an unclear priority. Matthew 6:33 is the God-given priority that has not changed. Follow it and your ministry will receive divine approval in Jesus' name.

Washing of Feet

How pathetic it is that the Lord's demonstration of humility has been taken literally. In the days of old, the door slaves in Israel used to be the lowest cadre of slaves. It was the responsibility of the door slave to wash the dust off the feet of visitors who came to his master's house. He sat outside the door with his basin of water performing this duty. Therefore when Jesus wanted to demonstrate true humility, he began to wash the feet of His disciples. As Israelites, they immediately understood the message behind the act, John

13:5-7. They understood that He was demonstrating to them that the leader should condescend to serve his followers, even up to the extent of the lowest and meanest service when necessary.

> *And so when He had washed their feet and taken His garments, and reclined at the table again. He said to them, 'do you know what I have done to you?'*
> *John 13:12 (NASB)*

Many have not answered this question. Some think that Jesus is recommending a practice called **the washing of feet,** in which the pastor takes water and a towel and washes the feet of every member of his congregation. Today some practice this and still harbor hatred and animosity against those whose feet they have washed. Shame on you that do this!

> *You call Me Teacher and Lord; and you are right, for so I am. If then, the Lord and the teacher wash your feet, you also ought to wash one another's feet for I gave you an example that you should do as I did to you. Truly, truly I say to you a slave is not greater than*

the one who sent him. If you know these things, you are blessed if you do them, John 13:13-17.

Was the Lord recommending that we should be literally washing one another's feet? No, please. He was simply demonstrating that the leader must be willing to humble himself to serve even those he is leading. Recall that His audience was only the twelve apostles whom he prepared as the leaders of the early Church. He was speaking to the leaders and not to the entire congregation.

It is unfortunate that today many Pentecostals have taken this practice of feet washing literally. Right in the church, pastors have used God's time of worship to literally wash the feet of the entire congregation. The devil has deceived you! This is the same as those who read Ecclestiasis 9:8 and then refuse to wear any other color of clothes except white. Understand what you read in the Bible, Acts 8:30.

Please repent. Christianity is not occultism. Stop striving to make it look like the idol worship of your fathers.

Faith in Christ is what is needed. Even the olive oil ministration is only used to boost the faith of those who are weak. If you believe enough in God, you need no oil. The prayer of faith is what saves the sick, have faith in God, and your faith will be richly rewarded in Jesus name, Mark 11:22

Christ's Fulfillment of the Law, Matt. 5:17-48

It is interesting to read about the way the Lord Jesus fulfilled the Law. If you read the passage through, you will see that the Lord referred to some of the Old Testament practices that did not fully fulfill God's purpose. He corrected us in order to fulfill God's purpose.

Let us see the examples.

> *You have heard that it was said to those of old 'You shall not murder, and whoever murders will be in danger of the judgment.' But I say to you that whoever is angry with his brother without a cause shall be in danger of the judgment. And whoever says to his*

> *brother, 'Raca!' shall be in danger of the council. But whoever says, 'You fool' shall be in danger of hell fire! Matt. 5:21-22*

Here the Lord is making us to know that murder is not just the physical act of killing but that one becomes guilty of the sin of murder the moment it is conceived in his heart.

> *You have heard that it was said to those of old 'You shall not commit adultery.' But I say to you that whoever looks at a woman to lust for her has already committed adultery with her in his heart, Matt. 5:27-28.*

Here the Lord clarifies that adultery is not just the physical act but that one becomes guilty the moment those lustful thought are accommodated in the heart. Clearly God is more interested in the state of the heart rather than the mere physical act. As evil and as conclusive as the physical act of sin may be, before God, man is found already guilty as soon as he permits those evil thoughts to overcome him in his heart. By this correction the Lord directs us to jealously guard the state of our hearts.

> *You have heard that it was said. 'An eye for and eye and a tooth for a tooth.' But I tell you not to resist an evil person. But whoever slaps you on your right cheek turn the other to him also, Matt.5: 38-39.*

Here the Lord refuted the **eye for an eye** law that operated in the time past. Jesus who came from the bosom of the Father has come to unfold to us what the mind of the Father is. Our resistance should not be by the human weapons of muscles, clubs and knives. But rather by the spiritual weapons that are far more effective.

> *If your enemy is hungry, give him bread to eat; and if he is thirsty, give him water to drink; for so you will heap coals of fire on his head and the Lord will reward you, Prov. 25:21-22.*

The days are gone when we are expected to avenge ourselves. Today the Lord requires that we leave the prerogative of vengeance to Him.

Bless those who persecute you; bless and do not curse. Repay no one evil for evil. Have regard for good things in the sight of all men…. Beloved, do not avenge yourselves, but rather give place to wrath for it is written, 'Vengeance is mine I will repay,' Says the Lord. Do not be overcome by evil but overcome evil with good,
Rom. 12:14, 17, 19 and 21

Not returning evil for evil or reviling for reviling but on the contrary blessing, knowing that you were called to this, that you may inherit a blessing,
1Peter 3:9

This is the spirit of the real child of God. Those who advocate physical violence are trying to propagate Christianity like Islam. Christianity is not a religion of physical force but rather of spiritual force. Call those spiritual forces to bear by creating a conducive environment for their activity; they will be harnessed to your favor. If you try to save yourself, you will not succeed. But if you surrender even your very life for Jesus' sake you will be calling into play the most effective power from God to ensure that your life is secure.

> *For whoever desires to save his life will lose it, and whoever loses his life for My sake will find it, Matt. 16:25*

Finally, the Lord releases to us the excellent principles of love in verses 43- 48.

> *You have heard that it was said, 'You shall love your neighbor and hate your enemy'. But I (Jesus)* say to you, love your enemies and (hear that),* bless those who curse you (including the witches and wizards)* do good to those who hate you and pray for those who spitefully use you and persecute you...*
> **Bracketed words mine*

Jesus cannot lead us astray. Jesus who made all things began by reminding us of how things were done previously. He then gave us the new mode of operation. Trust in God that no sorcery or curse can work against you – no matter who utters it. This is because Jesus has redeemed us from all curses. Therefore, we are above curses. By cursing back those who curse you, you do not revoke their own curse. The only reason that those curses will not work against you as a believer is because the blood of Jesus has justified you. And the law requires that there must be a **cause** for the curse to act on you. Every believer is however made free from all such causes.

> *Christ has redeemed us from the curse of the law having become a curse for us (for it written, 'Cursed is everyone who hangs on a tree.'), Gal. 3:13.*

> *Like a flitting sparrow, like a flying swallow so a curse without cause shall not alight, Prov. 26:2*

You cannot change God's words. Either you obey them or you don't. But if you are to be called a true child of God, you must resemble your father in heaven.

> *Therefore you shall be perfect, just as your Father in heaven is perfect, Matt. 5:48*

This is God's expectation of us, not that we should go about killing unbelievers of any category. What could have been our lot today if an over-zealous believer, whom we persecuted before we repented, had decreed our death? Definitely we would not have the hope we have today. Think about those believers who Paul was chasing about to arrest and imprison when he was yet Saul. If they had decreed his death, we would not now have the great benefits we have in the repentance of that mighty man of God. There would have been no Epistles of Paul today in the Bible. What a loss that would have been!

God has called us to save souls, not to destroy them. Do you not know that those who have been forgiven their great sins love more than those who have been forgiven little?

> *Therefore I say to you, her sins, which are many, are forgiven, for she loved much. But to whom little is forgiven, the same loves little, Luke 7:4 and 7*

Therefore, even in the most terrible sins, God's interest is to save man and not to destroy him.

Endure Persecution Matt. 10:16-26

Persecutions are coming. We are called to endure them and not to fight back.

> ***But I tell you not to resist an evil person, Matt. 5:39***

We are to be **harmless** and not violent to our persecutors. This is part of the price to be paid in order to inherit His Kingdom.

> ***Behold I send you out as sheep in the midst of wolves. Therefore be wise as serpents and harmless as doves, Matt. 10:16***

> ***Many are the afflictions of the righteous but the Lord delivers him from them all, Psalm 34:19***

He is the one that delivers us. We do not deliver ourselves.

> ***But you be watchful in all things, endure affliction, 2Tim. 4:5***

Being watchful in all things is the same as the call to be wise as a serpent. He knows that we are being thrown to the wolves and so he calls us to use our wits and to ***endure*** when affliction comes. Jesus endured affliction in His time. Paul the apostle, Peter, James, John, Silas, Barnabas, and all the New Testament saints endured persecutions and afflictions. In Acts 23:6-10, Paul was watchful and he showed us a good example of how to be ***wise as serpents*** in the time of affliction.

We are not to resist flesh and blood with physical violence. Resorting to physical violence is a sign of spiritual failure. In fact God has not authorized the use of any physical weapons for our warfare.

> ***For the weapons of our warfare are not carnal… 2Cor. 10:4.***

Ephesians 6:10-18 shows all the ammunitions approved for our use in the spiritual warfare confronting us as Christians. If God expects us to fight with flesh and blood, He would have approved some physical weapons for us to use to execute this aspect of the warfare. But He did not approve any physical weapons. Instead

He clearly tells us that our contention is not against flesh and blood, Eph. 6:12.

In fact He tells us **never** to quarrel with man but to be gentle to all (including unbelievers), 2Tim. 2:24. Look at the lives of the believers of old, after the Lord ascended into heaven. You will not find any single example of physical resistance to violence. They were flogged, beaten, harassed and afflicted in all kinds of ways. When Peter, who had cut off Marcus' ear at Gethsemane, caught the revelation of the truth of Jesus' teachings, he endured imprisonment, affliction and persecutions. Even the blessings promised to the believer here on earth is to be accompanied with persecution, Mark 10:29-30.

> *Yes and all who desire to live godly in Christ Jesus will suffer persecution, 2Tim. 3:12.*

Do you know that at a time, the believers were so numerous that they could have effectively challenged the opposition, physically? But the apostles never encouraged them to resist physically. Rather they used the all-powerful tool of prayer to contend with persecutions and afflictions, Acts 4:23-31, 5:40-42

Therefore, you need to fully make up your mind whether to follow the Bible example or human reasoning and teaching. But remember that human convictions are not the same as God's word. God says that we should endure afflictions and persecutions but man says that we should destroy the unbelievers and persecutors. And I say to you:

> ***Choose for yourselves this day whom you will serve. But as for me and my house, we will serve the Lord,***
> ***Josh. 24:15***

God has no pleasure in the death of a sinner, neither does He wish that any should perish but rather that all should come to repentance, Ezekiel 18:23, 2Peter 3:9. It is not an easy task to endure afflictions. That is why Jesus warns us to count the cost first before embarking on His follower-ship, Luke 14:28-30. When we do this, there comes a day of reward, which the Lord has prepared in His program. You may have to wait until then for your reward for enduring afflictions, Matt. 16:27. Meanwhile, the call today is for endurance.

> *But he who endures to the end shall be saved, Matt. 24:13*

Authority of the Church, Matt. 16:19

Although the Lord has taught us about the excellence of love and His expectations that we should endure persecution, He did not however leave us powerless. A very powerful tool has been given to the church.

> *And I will give you the keys of the kingdom of heaven, and whatever you bind on earth will be bound in heaven, and whatever you loose on earth will be loosed in heaven, Matt. 16:19.*

As we use this authority today, let us always remember that we are not wrestling against flesh and blood but against diabolic powers and spirits, Luke 10:19.

Let us not bind men but evil spirits. Let us not trample on men but on the diabolical spirits. A neglect of this is tantamount to operating contrary to God's will. Of course if we bind men, they will be bound, Matt. 18:19. But the law of the spirit of life prohibits us from doing this without being expressly led to do so by the Holy Spirit. We should help to save men, not to bind them, condemning them to perpetual doom. Let us use our God-given authority according to His will. A spiritual action is not justified just because it works. Therefore do not be advocating Christian violence on the grounds that it works. Of course, it will work. You have received the authority! But God trust that you will let the heart of Christ, which is a compassionate, loving and forgiving heart, be manifested in you. This is why power without purity is dangerous. No wonder the greater power of God is released to the believer only after he has become baptized in the Holy Spirit, Acts, 1:8. That way, the custodian does not become a deadly threat to others. There are however times when the Spirit of God uses this power, by His own motivation against evildoers (flesh and blood).

We see the case of Ananias and Sapphira in Acts 5:1-11. Peter spoke here ***by the Holy Spirit*** and the judgment was instant. As a result, great fear came upon all the Church and upon all who heard it.

The Lord Jesus Christ once used a cane to chase away moneychangers from God's temple, Mark 11:15-17. Also when Sergius Paulus the proconsul at the Island of Patmos invited Paul and Barnabas, Elymas, a sorcerer began to withstand them. But **Paul full of the Holy Spirit said,**

> *'O full of all deceit and all fraud, you son of the Devil, you enemy of all righteousness, will you not cease perverting the straight ways of the Lord? And now indeed the hand of the Lord is upon you and you shall be blind, not seeing the sun for a time.' And immediately a dark mist fell on him, and he went around seeking someone to lead him by the hand. Then the proconsul believed, when he saw what had been done, being astonished at the teaching,*
> *Acts 13:10-12.*

Of course immediately the man became blind, the proconsuls believed. It is interesting to note that in each of these cases, the apostles only pronounced judgments that were already passed in the spiritual realm *by the Holy Spirit*. They were simply the mouthpieces or instruments used by God to pronounce His judgments – '*And now indeed the hand of the Lord is upon you.*' Therefore, for you declare this authority on any flesh and blood, it should be only by the Holy Spirit's motivation. Of course the Holy Spirit is not bound by any limitations. He does what He wills. No man has the right to seek to either justify or condemn His actions. That is part of being God. He must therefore lead us before we raise our authority against any flesh and blood. At such times, you are not the one contending but the Spirit of your Father who is inside you is simply using you as an instrument of His expression to execute His will.

The Supremacy of Love, 1Cor. 13:1-8

One of the most pronounced attributes of our Lord Jesus Christ is love. He is our example. He came to show us who God really is, out of the bosom of God, John 1:18.

In each of His teachings on the fulfillment of the law as we saw in Matthew chapter 5, He began with the word.

> ***You have heard that it was said to those of old…but I say to you,***
> ***Matt. 5:21-22, 27-28, 31-34, 38-39, 43–44***

Therefore, you as a Christian today must follow what Jesus said and not what was said to those of old. That is the meaning of being a Christian – like Christ. The Holy Spirit continued this message of love when He spoke through Paul the apostle in 1Corinthians 13. Earlier in chapter 12 he had closed by saying:

> ***And yet I show you a more excellent way, 1Cor. 12:31***

Then He began to talk about love and its qualities. He condemned speaking in tongues, prophecy or giving of alms **without love.** He then went on to say:

> ***Love suffers long and is kind; love does not envy. Love does not parade itself, is***

not puffed up; does not behave rudely, does not seek its own; is not provoked, thinks no evil; does not rejoice in iniquity, but rejoices in the truth; bears all things, believes all things, hopes all thing. Love never fails, 1Cor. 13:4-8.

It will serve you much in imbibing these qualities if you daily read and meditate on this passage. This is true Christ-likeness in our application of our God-given authority. With these attributes, your spiritual defenses will become formidable and insurmountable. Then can you truly say:

"No weapon formed against **ME** *shall prosper..."*
Isaiah 54:17

When we give out love in this way, we will begin to enjoy Christianity. Joy that knows no bounds will become ours. Life on earth will be full of most interesting daily challenges as we explore fresh avenues of demonstrating our Christ-likeness. The world will begin to understand the power of Jesus in our lives. Needless to say that forgiveness is natural for a man of such love capacity. The true passion for souls will become evident in our lives. Our evangelistic ministries will spring out from loving and compassionate hearts. The Holy Spirit will have joy in using us when we are thus prepared. The extent of power manifestation in such hearts is tremendous.

You that seek for power, this is the way to prepare yourself and God will surely baptize you with great power that, without asking for it, men will fall down at your mere appearance. The blind will see at your touch, the lame will walk at your command, the barren will conceive at your word and the dead will rise up alive at your command. You will begin to know glimpses of the fullness of our God-given authority, which continually unfolds itself when we allow the purity of this Christ-like love to manifest in us. Do not be deceived. In the path of love, humility and obedience to God lies the greatest power at the disposal of man. He has promised that we shall do greater works than He did.

> *Most assuredly, I say to you, he who believes in Me the works I do he will also do; and greater works than these he will do, because I go to My Father*

and whatever you ask in My name, that I will I will do, that the Father may be glorified in the Son. If you ask anything in My name, I will do it,
John 14:12-14

One thing is sure: ***Love never fails, 1Cor. 13:8a.*** So, now that you have been reminded of the truth, decide never again to allow yourself to be deceived into going back to the old hatred, malice and un-forgiveness which you gave up when you first repented. Let the purity of the heart that is desired by God be manifested in you. Remember that it is the pure in heart who will see God, Matt.5: 8 The Lord will soon come and it will be unfortunate for you to be so engrossed in conflicts with evil men on earth that you are robbed of that one time opportunity to meet with your Lord. The pre-requisites to taking part in the Rapture have not changed. They are still, peace with all men and holiness, Heb. 12:14.

Husbands, love your wives, just as Christ also loved the church and gave Himself for it, that He might sanctify and cleanse it with the washing of water by the word that He might

> ***present it to Himself a glorious church, not having spot or wrinkle or any such thing, but that it should be holy and without blemish, Eph. 5:25-27.***

The church that Jesus will present to Himself in the Rapture is going to be a holy church. It will be a spotless, unwrinkled and unblemished church. In fact if there is any such thing as sin in your life at that very instant of the Rapture, you will miss it. No man with blemishes and spots will be presentable to the Lord on that day.

Therefore, make up your mind what your goal in life is. If it is to make the Rapture, then get into the boat of holiness because that is the one that sails to the heavenly Promised Land. But if you want to go to hell then go on with your careless Christianity. But remember that there is a risk that death may unexpectedly catch you in your unguarded hour of careless sinful living and you will end up on the hell end of the eternity fence. Do not allow false teachers to blind you to the truth. Let your heart ever be pure. It is the love of God that brings this timely message to you in order to prepare your heart for that day. The Day will come in the twinkling of an eye. Unexpectedly like a thief in the night, the Lord will come, Mark 13:32-33, 35-37, 1Thess. 5:1-2, 1Cor. 15:51-52.

The warning you will get is this book you are reading now. You must learn to live consistently in true Christian holiness, as a natural way of life and not that you are holding out to the end. Holiness is an act of faith (*see The Character of the Anointed).* When love is flowing through you, you will even begin to enjoy the trials.

> *My brethren, count it all joy when you fall into various trials, James 1:2.*

Let love have its unhindered way in your life, and you will truly know the days of heaven upon this earth, Deut. 11:21. The Lord Himself will uphold you in this path of love in Jesus name – Amen.

CHAPTER FOUR

UNDUE EXALTATION OF THE DEVIL

There is no doubt that the devil is a strong man. Our Lord Jesus Christ clearly described him as such.

> *When a strong man, fully armed, guards his own palace, his goods are in peace. But when a stronger than he comes upon him and overcomes him, he take from him all his armor in which he trusted, and divides his spoil, Luke 11:21-22*

Demons Consciousness

As you can see from the passage above, the Lord Jesus Christ is stronger than the devil. That is why we have victory over Satan and his cohorts. The Lord gave us authority over the devil before He returned to heaven, Luke 10:19. This authority is enough to make any believer fearless. But no, some will teach that we must live in fear of the devil. The Lord said **by any mean** and that means that as long as you are a member of the family of God, the devil is not permitted to touch you. And truly He confirms this in 1John 5:18,

> *We know that whoever is born of God does not sin; but who has been born of God keeps himself and the wicked one does not touch him.*

Keeping yourself especially involves keeping your faith. The moment you allow that devil to arrogate undue powers to himself, he has got you. Believe God that nothing shall by any means hurt you and it shall be so for you.

For as he thinks in his heart so is he, Prov. 23:7

You are of God, little children, and have overcome them, because He who is in you is greater than he who is in the world, 1 John 4:4

Because you are of God, you have overcome them. You have overcome the powers of darkness.

He has delivered us from the power of darkness and translated us into the kingdom of the Son of His love, Col. 1:13

Do you not know that God in His fullness is dwelling in you as a believer, John 14:15-18, 23? To ensure this, you should love God and keep His commandments. This is the human requirement in order to overcome the devil.

The Role of faith

But remember that without believing in Christ you can neither keep God's commandments nor do His work.

> ***Then they said to Him, 'what shall we do, that we may work the works of God?' Jesus answered and said to them, 'This is the work of God, that you believe in Him whom He sent, John 6:28-29.***

Anytime you fail to believe God and you believe the devil instead, anytime you fail to believe that God protects you as His own but you believe that the demons are after you and have powers over you, God is not pleased. The devil thus gains entrance because you have allowed him in by exercising fear rather than faith. Many actually have faith in the devil's ability to harm them, Gal. 2:20.

As Elisha said to his servant:

> ***Do not fear for those who are with us are more than those who are with them, 2Kings 6:16***

We have unseen spiritual forces on our side, dispatched to ensure our safety. These angelic forces deployed to minister to our needs are not in any way careless, Hebrew 1:13-14.

Moreover the eyes of our Father are perpetually on us, 1Peter 3:12.

Read Psalm 121 and understand the extent of God's care upon us His children. It does not matter what we see visibly. The truth is that **nothing shall by any means hurt** a true child of God who exercises unshakable faith in Him. Even though in our natural state, the devil was too strong for us, as soon as we become born-again and Jesus begins to dwell inside of us, God is committed by His own word to delivering us from Satan's hands.

> *For I, says the Lord, will be a wall of fire all around her (the church) and I will be a glory in her midst.*
> *Zech. 2:5*

> *He permitted no man to do them wrong; yes He reproved kings for their sakes saying, 'Do not touch my anointed ones and do my prophets no harm,' 2Chron. 16: 21-22.*

> *For thus says the Lord of hosts: He sent me after glory to the nations,*

which plunder you; for he who touches you touches the apple of His eyes,
Zech. 2:8

He delivered me from my strong enemy, from those who hated me; for they were too strong for me,
2Sam. 22:18.

They were too strong for me but now; I am too strong for them in Jesus name. Praise God! Do not allow the devil to convince you otherwise. He is a strong man all right but to us he is rather weak. A dog is a strong animal but compared to a lion, it is a weakling.

Yet in all things we are more than conquerors through Him (Jesus)* who loved us, Rom. 8:37.
*Bracketed words mine

The moment you catch the revelation in your spirit that all of God, including all his power and resource, is in you, you will begin to feel his strength coursing through your spirit-man. Divine power will be spontaneously released within you and barriers of your limitations will crumble like Jericho walls. Then will the saying come to pass in you that,

> ***...but the people who know their God shall be strong and carry out great exploits, Dan. 11:32***

So now that you know how powerful and strong you really are, it is time for great exploits for the Lord. Never again let yourself become devil-conscious. Do not give the devil any undue recognition, in yours prayers, in your daily living or in your ministry. He is not after you. Even though as your adversary, he is walking about like a roaring lion seeking whom he may devour, if you resist him steadfast in the faith, he will flee from you, 1Peter 5:8-9; James 4:7

This means that the devil will run from you in fear. It is the weaker that runs away from the stronger, not vice versa. So refuse to play the weakling to the devil. Be on the offensive against Satan and the power of darkness. God is in you. Remember that at the name of Jesus every knee shall bow, Rom 14:11.

Resolve never to be a reproach to God and the church by suffering defeat from the hand of the devil. It is a spiritual battle fought in the faith realm. When you begin to recognize that adverse situations and circumstances are actually God at work in His wondrous ways in answer to your prayers, then you can give thanks to Him in everything. You should be convinced that all things truly work together for your good as one of those who love God, Rom 8:28.

Is God striving with the devil? He is not at all. God is too strong for the devil. Once you have an unshakable faith in God, then even in your trials, your spirit will be full of joy, James 1:2.

Resolve ever to be God-conscious and never demon-conscious for demons are defeated foes. When they rise up, remind them about the victory of Calvary through spiritual warfare in prayer. They simple will flee in terror.

The Use of the Blood of Jesus

Many believers now apply the blood of Jesus in a fetish manner, like the concoctions of a sorcerer. As a result of the fear that has eroded their faith, the blood of Jesus has become their talisman. When their fear returns, they plead the blood of Jesus. In fact the life span of their faith is so brief and the pleading of the blood of Jesus has become a kind of recharging of the battery of their faith. Brethren these things ought not to be so. If you have no faith, why not go and give quantity time to hearing the word of God so that faith will come, Rom.10: 17. You can use anointed, faith-building cassette messages to achieve this, if there is no means of immediate fellowship.

Do you not know that fear brings torments? 1John 4:18

Your Christian life will not have the joy that liberty brings if you live in fear. Maybe you are now a bottled-up nervous wreck living in perpetual fear of the devil and his cohorts. Relax, for God took control as soon as you prayed. That prayer you made in the morning asking God to take care of your day, He heard it. Recall that He has charged us not to be worried about life:

Be anxious for nothing, but in everything by prayer and supplication, with thanksgiving let your requests be made known to God, Phil. 4:6.

When you requested for His protection, He heard you because it is prayer according to His will, Psalm 91:1. The confidence we have is that any prayer we make according to His will is an answered prayer, 1John 5:14-15.

So why are you fretting about, pleading the Blood of Jesus intermittently? Is it not a betrayal of your lack of faith? Where then is your faith? You can never substitute faith with the blood of Jesus. The blood of Jesus has its unique role to play in the spiritual scheme of things, such as purification, justification, and sanctification. For the right purpose and time, if you use the blood of Jesus, you will see the tremendous power that it packs.

Authoritative Prayer Attitude

When binding demonic powers, our attitude must be that of a conviction that our orders are being obeyed. It becomes necessary to repeat orders when you are unsure that the first order was obeyed. This could be because the person who was ordered did not hear the order, did not understand the order or simply refused to obey. Repetition of an order is only necessary to ensure that the order is heard or understood. But where obedience was refused, you should rather find out why your orders were not obeyed. Then you should take proper corrective measures to ensure future obedience than to waste time and energy shouting repetitive orders. If faith is lacking as you issue decrees, then be sure that you will get no results no matter how loud you shout. But when you have faith as a result of having heard from God, your confidence is mountain moving and useful result invariably follows.

When you bind the same spirits many times on the same day, is it not an acknowledgement that you doubt that these demons have been properly bound? Look, your error is in allowing the devil to erode your faith. When the disciples of the Lord had a similar problem, when they tried unsuccessfully to cast out a mute and an epileptic spirit from a boy, Jesus replied, in answer to the reason for their failure:

> *...O faithless generation, how long shall I be with you. How long shall I bear with you? Mark 9:19*

When you have bound the devil and he comes back putting doubts in you, the answer is in the word of God. Use the Scriptures to anchor your faith. Tell the devil: ***It is written.***

Tell him what the Bible, which is our battle manual, has to say about the issue at stake. Give the devil scriptural reasons why he is totally powerless in your hands. Jesus used it in Matt. 4:1-11 to show us an example. When you have such a verbal exchange with the devil, it is called a spiritual battle. You are to fight at that time with the whole armor of God, Eph. 6:10- 18. This is how to wrestle with diabolical spirits. It takes place in the thought realm. Between you and Satan, spiritual battles are fought and won on a daily basis. You should have your armory full of spiritual weapons so that you may be able to withstand whenever the devil comes to challenge your rights. If you do not know these rights by a regular reading of the Bible, chances are that the devil will defeat you and you may now resort to shouting the Blood of Jesus in order to scare away the offensive devil. For how long will you continue to live this way? Deal with the situation once and for all and receive your due spiritual promotion that comes as an aftermath of victory over the adversary. May the Lord give you the grace to arise and overcome in Jesus' name?

Vain Repetition in Prayer, Matt. 6:7

At one time or another in the process of our spiritual growth, as a result of ignorance of the ways of God, we make God to appear to be hard to please. In our hearts we have determined that we shall continue to pray to God who may eventually be persuaded to help us even though what we ask of Him are proper and legitimate needs in our lives. As a result of ignorance of the superior knowledge of our Maker, we now appear before Him as the **righteous** down-trodden, while the Holy One of Israel appears to be the reluctant, frightful, unfeeling and sometimes even Wicked One. How terrible is the fact that sometimes our wrong attitudes have robbed us of our deserved victory. Please, get one fact through to your head: ***God is good!*** It does not matter what you are passing through. He is good,

Nah. 1:7. God does not have to answer your prayers according to your dictates. You cannot impose your will on Him. Although He loves us, He knows our ignorance and He answers the prayers of all His millions of children. Sometimes our requests are in conflict with one another. I could pray for rain while you pray for drought for the same place and at the same time. It takes a superior intelligence to answer both prayers. He however gives us the assurance that He causes all things to work together for good to them that love Him. So watch your heart! Never you hate or despise God. Never speak against Him even when the going appears roughest.

A study of the model for prayer taught by our Lord Jesus Christ in Matt. 6:13 shows that prayer does not just consist in petition or supplication. In fact a greater part of prayer is given to worship, adoration, praises, thanksgiving and the call for the establishment of His will on earth. When you have made known your request to God, your prayer subsequently should be concentrated in the affirmation of God's divine ability in meeting these needs. Speak His words back to Him. It serves the dual purpose of both establishing the irrevocability of the answer to your prayer as well as strengthening your own faith. When you remind God of His never-failing words, He is provoked into action and your answer comes speedily. It is like letting the powers that be know that you know your rights. In the spiritual realm, there are many forces at play both for and against us, 2King 6:1, Dan.10: 10-13, 20. But then, we are God's special treasure. We are especially privileged as sons of God, co-heir with the Lord Jesus Christ. Our position in the spiritual realm is far above where the principalities and powers of the universe are. Therefore, when we declare unto the powers, our authority in the name of Jesus, they all bow and our rights are established, enforced, Exodus 10:5-6.

> ***But you are a chosen generation, a royal priesthood, a holy nation, His own special people, that you may proclaim the praises of Him who called you out of darkness into His marvelous light; who once were not a people but are now the people of God; who had not obtained mercy but now have obtained mercy, 1Peter 2:9-10.***

God declared through Moses what He was going to bring to pass in the new covenant. These prophecies have now been fulfilled in us in this dispensation. Apostle Peter revealed that we are now all those things that Moses prophesied that we should be. Get this revelation into your spirit by a meditation on God's promises for us today and you will find that your life will simply change to conform to their prophecy.

> ***For as he thinks in his heart so is he, Prov. 23:7***

When these revelations have sunk into you and they are firmly established in you, you are then able to confront the spiritual oppositions to your success and to let them know with authority who you really are, according to the unchanging word of God. Since there is no power that can successfully oppose the Word of God, ***'It is written'*** or ***Jesus***, these powers simply bow out of your life. Life becomes fun to the man who is set free through the knowledge of the truth, which is Christ.

> ***Therefore God also has highly exulted***

Him and given Him the name which is above every name that at the name of JESUS every knee should bow of those in heaven, and of those on earth, and of those under the earth, and that every tongue should confess that Jesus Christ is Lord, to the glory of God the Father, Phil. 2:9-11.

As a born-again child of God, be sure that you are in good relationship with your Father. You do this by keeping your covenant of righteousness, by being free from sin. As long as you are thus a member in good standing of God's family, never forget that His eyes are perpetually open to see you and His ears are open to hear all your prayers.

For the eyes of the Lord are on the righteous and His ears are open to their prayers… 1Peter 3:12.

Repeating the same thing over and over again is like praying like the heathen who think that they will be heard for their many words.

But when you pray, do not use vain repetitions as the heathen do. For they

think they will be heard for their many words, Matt. 6:7.

The Lord said in Luke 18:1.

Men always ought to pray and not lose heart.

What He means here is that you must not give up when you do not see the manifestation of the answer to your prayers. Do not give up praying, claiming that prayers do not work. That is losing heart. Also Paul said in 1Thess. 5:17,

Pray without ceasing.

It means that you should not give up on prayers. You should not cease praying. But you should *continue* to acknowledge God's ability to meet your needs. There gets a level in your Christian growth when you are always conscious of being in His presence. At this time you would have actualized Paul's charge to pray without ceasing. Then you may find yourself to be praying even as you are eating, bathing, playing, studying, conversing or going through the normal course of your daily life. You will successfully pray thus yet without paying half attention to daily living. There will be no bondage or infringement on your Christian liberty. Prayer at this time is an act of love for God. The soul perpetually yearns for nearness with God without satisfaction.

> *Now the Lord is the Spirit; and where the Spirit of the Lord is, there is liberty, 2Cor. 4:17.*

There are some people I know, who shut themselves up in a room whenever they are fasting and praying. They only emerge when they are over with it. This is wrong and the Bible condemns it. Clearly when the Lord was describing the proper attitude in fasting He said:

> *But you, when you fast, anoint your head and wash your face, so that you do not appear to men to be fasting but to your father who is in the secret place; and your Father who sees in secret will reward you openly, Matt.6: 17-18.*

This indicates that when you are fasting, you are actually exposed for men to see your face. You are not to go into solitary confinement of one or a few days. Even when the Lord was praying at Gethsemane for three hours, He broke the prayers up into hourly segments. In between, He went to meet and commune with His prayer partners, Matt. 26:36-46. God condemns the attitude of afflicting oneself in fasting and prayer, thereby painting a picture of appeasement of a reluctant God. God is not an idol and must not be treated as such in our hearts or in our attitudes, Isaiah 58:5. The danger in this wrong attitude in fasting is that God does not even accept the fasting. Man has not yet understood God but rather he is ever striving to make God fit into his man-made image of Him. God is good! Amen.

Adverse Circumstances and God's Purpose

Sometimes after prayers, we find that the situation deteriorates the more. There are times that we fast and pray and are convinced that God will intervene in our favor but suddenly a new development that appears to contradict our expectations comes into the situation.

Recently I had an encounter that God used to teach me quite a few lessons about Himself. I had applied to our Federal Ministry of Finance for Approval to remit foreign exchange. The ministry requested that I should bring an Agreement Letter between my company and the Oversea suppliers. I expected to get a reply within a few days so that I could conclude the whole transaction by the next week. I prayed well and sent off my fax message. Sure enough in a few days I got a reply but for some reason there was a lot of distortion from the fax system and the reply was partly illegible and so useless to serve my purpose. I sent another message back to my suppliers explaining the error and they sent me another reply saying:

> "We have prepared the following letter of agreement you requested. We will send you the original via express mail."

That was all I got. The Letter of Agreement itself, which was the vital document I needed, never came through by fax. I felt so disappointed. At that stage in my life, so much appeared to depend upon my success in getting through with that project. I had prayed to God as I knew how to. I felt betrayed. One thing I was sure of was that God could do all things. But my problem was in understanding why He did not just go ahead to do this one particular thing for me, Heb. 11:6.

Finally the express mail arrived and promptly I sent it off by courier to the ministry at Abuja about six hundred kilometers away. According to our previous arrangement, I was to take a follow-up trip to Abuja a week later by which time the Approval, if granted, would have been ready. A week later I had not succeeded in raising enough money for that trip. Finally on the tenth day I got enough and took off to Abuja. I traveled by road throughout that Tuesday and booked into a hotel on arrival. I could ill-afford the hotel bill at Suleja. Next morning I proceeded to the Ministry at Abuja only to hear on arrival that there was a nationwide labor strike in protest against the government removal of fuel subsidy. As a result, the regular staff of the Ministry did not come to work and no one knew how long the strike would last.

Imagine how I felt. Surely God knew about the impending strike action. Why then did He not let my fax reply get to me earlier as I had asked of Him in prayer? Why did He not at least prevent my journey in order to save me the wasted expenses? Better still, He could have deferred the strike action until after my visit. After all, He is God and can do all things. I had prayed to Him and trustingly committed the trip into His hands. Why did he fail me?

As I stood there too dazed to decide on what to do next, the lone security man on duty interrupted my thought.

> "If you want to see the Director, he is on seat," he said.

See the Director? That was an incredible opportunity. Off course if the normal work staff were on duty, seeing the Director would have been a feat of its own. I gave him my card and sure enough, I was invited up. As I got into the spaciously furnished office, I was surprised to meet a rather nice-looking and amiable gentleman who was the Director. Briefly I outlined my need and sure enough he explained how helpless he was as a result of the strike action. At this point, the Holy Spirit took over my tongue. I found myself explaining the details of the project for which I sought approval from his Ministry.

I showed him my feasibility study and explained in great detail how the nation shall benefit from the project. When I finished, I discovered surprising that I had a most attentive and impressed audience. The man swung into action. He said that mine was the kind of project that they were committed to assist and promote. He promised that if he found my file with them, then I would surely return that same day with the approval. I felt sure then that God would show him where my file was. But no! Every effort made to locate my file proved abortive. Of course you know I felt once again betrayed by a tantalizing God.

From there I went to Lagos to await the end of the strike action. When this happened, I called the Director who was by then on first name terms with me. He asked me to come over with my papers. Again it took me nearly one week to raise enough money for the trip. But when I got to Abuja that Monday morning, his secretary told me that I could see him only for a minute as he crossed into his office to prepare for their usual Monday meetings which would last almost the whole day.

As I went to thank him for his assistance, he explained that since our last meeting, he had given serious consideration to my project and had in partnership with some influential men from his State decided to appoint me as a consultant to establish a similar project for them, train their staff and see the project through to a successful execution. I was asked to name my consultancy fee. Just like that!

I was overwhelmed. Do you now see why God did not allow them to get to my file that first day? It was in order to give the man time to consider the project and make the proposal to me. I suddenly realized what the Lord meant when he said.

> ***Now to him who is able to do exceedingly abundantly above all we ask or think according to the power that works in us, to Him be glory in the church by Christ Jesus throughout all ages, world without end. Amen. Eph. 3:20-21***

He did for me exceedingly abundantly above the approval that I asked for and gave me so much more than I thought or imagined. God is good! In the process of His answered prayers, the circumstances may appear totally adverse but please know it that it is God at work. My experience and testimony is akin to that of biblical Joseph who was sold into slavery, sent to serve Potiphar as a slave and then slammed into jail, but at the appointed time, events began to take shape to bring about a fulfillment of God's declared intention to make him a ruler over his brethren. Moreover, through these apparently adverse circumstances, Israel was saved from famine. God is good!

What is your situation today? Does it appear as though even God is against you? Does He appear to have allowed the devil to have the upper hand in your situation? I say to you like Joseph of old said: The devil may mean evil against you, "But God meant if for good in order to bring it about…"Gen. 50:20.

For My thoughts are not your thoughts, nor are your ways My ways,'

> *say the Lord. 'For as the heavens are higher than the earth, so are My ways higher than your ways and My thoughts than your thoughts,"*
> *Isaiah 55:8-9*

Let us simply make our requests known to Him and forget the anxieties. He really cares for us and has asked that we should cast all our cares upon Him for He cares for us, I Peter 5:7. When we have done this, let us not go back trying to get God to solve the problem ***our way***. Cast your cares upon Him and leave the cares there with Him. He can handle it. But it may not be your way. Anyway, if your way were the right way of handling it, you would not have needed to come to Him. So having failed, why not let God do it His way. Sometimes His way appears to be the opposite of your expectations. But do not worry. Eventually His way always proves to be the best way to achieve, even better than, your expected result. Next time you pray and you begin to perceive adverse circumstance apparently at work, learn to see every adverse circumstance as a stepping-stone to your success. Israel was not led by a direct route but by a roundabout route out of Egypt to Canaan – the Promised Land.

His Prerogative of Time, Acts 1:7

Time is one element that tries every believer sorely. Man is an impatient creature naturally. But God wants us to acquire patience. In fact He introduces trails in our lives sometimes in order to perfect us in patience.

> ***My brethren, count it all joy when you fall into various trials knowing that the testing of your faith produces patience. But let patience have its perfect work, that you may be perfect and complete, lacking nothing." James 1:2-4***

Our attitude as such times must be one of joy. Sometimes God reveals His time- table to us but this is the exception rather than the rule. If He reveals this to you, do not joke with the vision. Follow it through and you will see it realized. If however He does not, never quit trusting Him. Eventually He will perform it. In fact the right word is that eventually He will finish it. This is because as soon as you asked Him He began doing it according to His own way. If you persist in your confession of God's divine ability to do these things and in your faith in Him, soon enough, He will answer you- speedily. Actually He answered as soon as you prayed, but certain spiritual circumstances bring about the manifestation of the answer in due season. But be assured that God is never late in manifesting His answered prayers. Failure only comes when faith is lacking. That is the message of Luke 18:1-8 (Note especially verse 8).

Our Response

Now that the truth has been revealed to you, resolve to retrace your steps. If you have sinned in blaming God unjustly due to your lack of understanding of His ways, ask Him for forgiveness. I did that too when I was having the experience that I have just testified to you. Blaming God causes spiritual stagnation. When you are sorely tried, God is about to promote you. But if you blame God, at the time of your trial, even in the secret place of your heart, you may have to repeat your trial until you pass – that is until you learn never to blame God but to trust Him no matter the odds. If you continue to blame God when trial times come, it is like failing a particular examination and re-sitting it many times. In the spiritual realm, promotion will come only when you pass. Therefore spiritual promotion and growth will come only when you have learnt to glorify God in that situation of life. I blamed God for apparent adverse situations that I faced. But one night He spoke to me revealing to me what He was working at achieving in me: unshakable trust in God. I came to understand Him even before the testimony was finally fulfilled. I thank God for the opportunity to testify of His goodness towards me so that others may learn from my experience and enjoy the benefit of a joyous receiving of expectations from God.

> *For I know the thoughts that I think towards you,' says the Lord, 'thoughts of peace and not of evil, to give you a future and a hope. Jer. 29:11*

Above all things God's wish for His beloved children is that of prosperity and good health as they prosper spiritually, 3John 1:2. God is good! Never allow yourself to be deceived into thinking otherwise.

Our best prayer to God after making our request and petition should be:

Let Thy will be done in our lives.

When you surrender thus to Him, give thanks to Him in all situations and circumstances because, of a truth, all things work together for your own good! Rom 8:28.

CHAPTER FIVE

PRESENT DAY MISUSE OF THE OLD COVENANT

Have you ever wondered that despite your faithfulness in paying tithe yet you do not see the windows of heaven open to "pour out for you such blessings that there will not be room enough to receive it," as it was promised in Malachi 3:8-12

The reason for it is quite simple: that covenant of God has been made obsolete. It has been replaced by a new covenant. Therefore the promise in Malachi is no longer backed up by God in this dispensation and so does not work for us today. The apparent reward that you received for paying tithe is the normal harvest that you reap whenever you sow.

Some church leaders still insist on the use of the tithe law to provide for their needs. Some of these do so out of a lack of the knowledge of God's dealing with man according to dispensations. They are like some white garment churches today that still insist on offering animal sacrifices as prescribed in the Levitical laws. But there are, however, some church leaders that still insist on tithes in this dispensation because of the huge material benefits that accrue personally to them from it. They are reluctant to tell the truth to their followers. I will tell it to you now and also show you from the word of God so that you will be freed from their bondage. Fear not, the truth shall make you free.

> ***And you shall know the truth, and the truth shall make you free.***
> ***John 8:32***

Yet there are a few leaders that insist on tithes

due to ignorance. They have been taught to receive tithes and they simply practice it without proper verifications from God's word. It is unfortunate that the teachers of today in Christianity usually choose to teach the truth as it favors them. Otherwise how would you justify the fact that the same teacher who advocates freedom from legality in Christianity would also adamantly insist that his followers obey the legal requirements of the tithe law in this dispensation?

In the law, God gave us the means of prosperity. The law forced us to sow a certain percentage of our income, ten percent. By obeying this law, we were compelled to see the reward of the harvest. After the cross, we became freed from the legal requirements of the law. But even though we are free from its legal impositions, we are supposed to have been taught the righteousness imbedded in the law. All the righteous requirements of the law are to be fulfilled without bringing in the legality that is in the law. This is how to practice real Christian liberty.

Thus, the tithe law that stipulates ten percent gives way to the spiritual law of ***sowing and***

reaping, which has no stipulated proportion. But the requirement of the law in this instance is ten percent. Therefore we are taught not to sow less than ten percent, but rather to sow more, knowing and recognizing the spiritual principles at work: ***the more you sow, the more you reap*** and vice versa. This is the truth of the apostle's doctrine and this is what we should teach the church today. This is the reason that the early disciples even sold their properties and goods and brought their proceeds to the apostles' feet. Instead of bringing in ten percent, some even brought all. They were free to bring to the church whatever they were led by the Spirit of God to bring in.

It is also note-worthy that Ananias and Sapphira died because they did not bring in all the proceeds of the sale of their property, which they had pledged. They did not die because they brought less than ten percent.

Thus, there is no record in the Scripture of the early apostolic church ever paying tithes. Yet there are abounding records of how money and resources for the up-keep of the apostles were raised by the church.

The Bible is a progressive spiritual revelation. God unfolds His truth in the Bible in stages, in dispensations. Any attempt by believers today to live by any of the laws will also require that they live completely by *all* the law.

> *And I testify again to every man who receives circumcision that he is under obligation to keep the whole law. You have been severed from Christ you who are seeking to be justified by law; you have fallen from grace.*
> *Gal. 5:3-4*

In this dispensation, we are to live by grace. Grace however does not nullify the law but rather fulfills it. Fulfillment of the law by grace involves fulfilling the righteous requirement in the law without going along with the legality. Grace works through faith, (Eph. 2:8).

> *You foolish Galatians, who has bewitched you? This is the only thing I want to find out from you! Did you receive the Spirit by the works of the law or by hearing with faith? Are you so foolish? Having begun by the spirit,*

are you now being perfected by the flesh? Does He then who provides you with the Spirit and works miracles among you, do it by the works of the law or by hearing with faith... For as many as are of the works of the law are under a curse; for it is written, 'Cursed is everyone who does not abide by all things written in the book of the law to perform them.' Now, that no one is justified by the law before God is evident; for 'the righteous man shall live by faith.' However, the law is not of faith; on the contrary, 'He who practices them shall live by them.' Gal. 3:1-5, 10-12

Therefore knowing that we are in the grace dispensation, you cannot go back to the tithe, which is in the law. That would be like going back to offering bulls and sheep sacrifices today just because it is written in the Bible.

The Old Covenant Stated

We see a record of Abram paying tithe to Melchizedek in Genesis 14:18-20.

Then Melchizedek king of Salem brought out bread and wine, he was the priest of God Most High and he blessed him and said; "Blessed be Abram of God Most High, Possessor of heaven and earth; and blessed be God Most High, who has delivered your enemies into your hand; And he gave him a tithe of all. Gen. 14:18-20

The Holy Spirit in Hebrews 7 and 8 later explained this issue clearly. A thorough study of these passages will help you understand the mind of God today on this issue of tithe. In the Old Testament, God commanded the tithe of your profits (of your increase) to be given to the Levites, the strangers, the fatherless and the widows, Deut. 26:12-13. This portion of one's increase was holy to God, belonging to Him and was supposed to be removed from your house, Deut. 26:12-13. It was to be given to the different people mentioned earlier. No wonder He said that it was robbery to withhold the tithe and offering from His storehouse. The tithe was the sacred portion that belonged to God. It was never theirs to *give*. Rather they were to *bring* it into God's house. That was why He called then thieves that failed to bring what belonged to God back into God's house.

> *Will a man rob God? Yet you are robbing Me! But you say, 'How have we robbed thee?' In tithes and offerings.   Mal.   3:8   (NASB)*

Also we read from the book of Hebrews:

> *And indeed those who are of the sons of Levi who receive the priesthood, have a commandment to receive tithes, from the people according to the law, that is from their brethren… Heb. 7:5*

All these point to the fact that the tithe was part of the old covenant. It was supposed to be given to the sons of Levi who had received the priesthood. But for the believers of today however, we have all received the priesthood as many of us as are born again according to the prophecy spoken by the mouth of Moses.

> *And you shall be to me a kingdom of priest… Exodus 19:6*

And from Jesus Christ, the faithful witness, the first born of the dead and the ruler of the kings of earth to Him who loves us and released us from our sins by His blood, and He has made us to be a kingdom, priests to His God and Father ... Rev. 1:5-6 (NASB)

And thou hast made them to be a kingdom and priests to our God... Rev. 5:10 (NASB)

But you are a chosen race, a royal priesthood, a holy nation, a people for God's possession... 1 Peter 2:9 (NASB)

Who therefore should pay tithe to whom in the Body of Christ? In Christ Jesus we are all one. No part of the body is to be neglected but the members should have the same care for one another.

For even as the body is one and yet has many members but now there are many members but one body.... And there should be no division in the body, but that the members should have the same care for one another.

1Cor. 12:12-13, 20, 25 (NASB)

So, although God has appointed apostles, prophets, teachers etc. in the Body of Christ, He clearly tells us that we are one and that we should have the same care for one another. Why then would a part of the Body of Christ arrogate to itself the right to receive tithes from the rest of the Body when we are one with equal access to God today? It was in demonstration that we all have equal access to God today that the veil covering the Holy of Holies split in two at the death of the Lord Jesus Christ.

Whatever collections are made in the church ought to be for the work of ministry, to take care of the needy orphans and widows in the church and to provide for those who are in the work of providing spiritual food for the church. Equal care must be maintained in the church.

Church collection is not collection for the pastor. As the pastor provides spiritual food, he is entitled to the material things provided through collection. But that does not mean that one should dump the church treasury in the lap of the pastor to do with it as he wills, all in this claim of being a Levite.

No place in the Bible is a call into the five-fold ministry referred to as the Levitical priesthood. These are two different ministries in two different dispensations. Equating them only leads to the error of putting new wine into old wine skin. The Lord said that the skin would surely burst.

As a correspondence, Levitical priesthood in the present dispensation is synonymous with a call to the new birth. When one is born again he becomes a member of the kingdom of priests prophesied by Moses.

> *And you shall be to Me a kingdom of Priests, Exodus 19:6*

In support of this is the promise God made to prophet Jeremiah that He will multiply His Levitical priests as the host of heaven and as the sand of the sea.

> *As the host of heaven cannot be numbered nor the sand of the sea*

measured, so will I multiply... the Levites who minister to Me. Jer. 33:22

Therefore God is not talking about multiplying those he has called into the five-fold ministry but rather he is talking about multiplying the number of believers who are all priests called into the royal priesthood of 1 Peter 2:9. Is it not the same promise that God made to Abraham after his faith was proved?

Indeed I will greatly bless you and I will greatly multiply your seed as the stars of the heaven and as the sand, which is on the seashore; and your seed shall possess the gate of their enemies. Gen. 22:17

Certainly God was not talking about multiplying the Levites of old or those in the pastoral ministry, to that extent. But yes, the seed of Abraham, which is the Body Christ, can be perceived to be claiming that promise of old today. Follow the Scriptures progressively and know the dispensation where we are now. A Levite was born a Levite as one is born again a believer. The apostles of old were called into the five-fold ministry just as Aaron was called into the priesthood. There was equal care in the Body. That Body has not changed today. It is still the Body of Christ.

Jesus Example, Matt. 23:23

> ***Woe to you Scribes and Pharisees, hypocrites. For you pay tithe of mint and anise and cumin and have neglected the weightier matters of the law, justice and mercy and faith. These you ought to have done without leaving the other undone. Matt. 23:23***

From this passage the Lord appears to be supporting that believers of today should not neglect to pay their tithe. You should however recall that the time of Christ before His death on the cross was still in the old dispensation. At His death, the change was effected, the temple veil was torn apart and it was at this point that He wiped out the handwriting of legal requirements that were against us which were contrary to us. And He has taken them out of the way having nailed them to the cross. Col. 2:14. The cross marks the transition from the old to the new covenant.

Recall that after He healed a certain leper, He even told him to go and show himself to the priest and offer the necessary sacrifice prescribed by Moses, Matt 8:1-4. Leviticus Chapter 14 gives the details of the sacrifices required by the law for the cleansing of a leper. It involved sacrifices such as birds, wood, scarlet string, hyssop, lambs and flour. If you try that today, you will be declared a cultic idolater. But Jesus prescribed that the leper He had healed should go and do it because that law was still in force before Jesus went to the cross.

Even at His birth, recall that the prescribed old covenant sacrifices were properly offered on behalf of Jesus, Luke, 2:21- 24. In this instance, it was a sacrifice of a turtledove and two pigeons. Therefore when He told the Scribes and Pharisees, 'these things you ought to have done,' He was referring to this practice in its proper time frame. At that time the Scribes and the Pharisees were the custodians of the Mosaic Law and so were sitting on the seat of Moses who represents the law. The whole of Matthew chapter 23 with all its seven woes was directed at these custodians of the law. At the beginning of the chapter, the Lord started by identifying the subjects of His curse.

> ***Then Jesus spake to the multitude, and to His disciples saying, 'The Scribes and the Pharisees seat in Moses seat.'***
> ***Matt. 23:1-2(KJV)***

Having identified the Scribes and the Pharisees as sitting on the seat of the law, He began to berate them. This tirade ran through to verse 23 where He made reference to tithe. Finally in verse 36, He announced a very important end to this undesirable situation of the Pharisees.

> ***Verily I say unto you, all these things shall come upon this generation.***
> ***Matt. 23:36 (KJV)***

Here the Lord clearly shows that He deals with us in dispensations. The generation of the Scribes and Pharisees was the generation of tithing, the generation of the law. Tithing was never a Christian practice in the apostolic era. Neither is there a single record of these early believers offering tithe to their leaders. What we see is rather a selfless communal loving relationship among the brethren, Acts 2:44-47.

This resulted in there being a daily distribution among them according to individual needs. When problem arose as a result of neglect, the apostles promptly gave this job of distribution to a select few and the rest continued uninterrupted in their singular goal of ministering the word and prayer. Thus this precious word was able to reach you and me today Acts 6:1-6.

> *And the congregations of those who believed were of one heart and soul, and not one of them claimed that anything belonging to him was his own; but all things were common property to them. And with great power the apostles were giving witness to the resurrection of the Lord Jesus and abundant grace was upon all. For there was not a needy person among them, for all who were owners of land or house would sell them and bring the proceeds of the sales, and lay them at the apostles' feet; and they would distribute to each, as any had need.*
>
> *And Joseph, a Levite of Cyprian birth, who was also called Barnabas by the*

> *apostles (which translated means, son of encouragement), and who owned a tract of land, sold it and brought the money and laid it at the apostles' feet. Acts 4:32-37(NASB)*

We see in this passage that Joseph, a Levite who, according to the law, was supposed to receive tithes from the apostles, laid the proceeds of the sale of his land at the apostles' feet. Here the Bible demonstrated that the believers of old were not operating according to the Old Covenant law of the tithe but according to the New Covenant in Christ Jesus, which dictates that there should be equal care for every part of the body of Christ. Today this vital message has been neglected because of the erroneous teachings of the leaders of the Body of Christ. Let us return to the path walked by the saints of old so that revival may come. We are a kingdom of priests today with equal access to God's throne. The five-fold ministry is not the Levitical priesthood. But we are all priests to our God with equal right to offer sacrifices of praise and prayer to God.

But what situation do we find today? We see some church leaders today with doubtful calls whose sole aim and testimony is self-enrichment through the tithes of their members. Is it then surprising that their teachings and messages are solely based on material prosperity? Who hears about holiness and the rapture of the saints anymore in our churches? They either talk about deliverance from doubtful powers which sometimes originate from they themselves or they talk about material prosperity. I say to them: ***shame on you!*** One day they will render an account to the Lord. Out of the multitude that we see in their churches today, what percentage is genuinely saved and ready to be caught up in the clouds if the Lord were to come this minute? Rather than give the people the soul-saving messages that will fulfill the purpose of their calling, if they have a calling, they have resorted to being commercialized preachers. Truly their god is their belly and the evil prophesied in the Scriptures is being fulfilled on them, 2 Tim, 3:1-9.

If you find yourself guilty of the charges above, I urge you to repent and begin to speak the truth. Even if it means retracting your words, do so and God who has brought this message to you today shall keep your flock from deserting you. Let me remind you that God has His own ordained way by which His ministers shall be provided for in this dispensation. It is a spiritual and faith way, which ensures that we are even better provided for than when we deceive for personal gains. I pray that God will give you the needed courage to follow the truth and be set free. May your ministry receive the life of Christ by the Holy Spirit as you obey God in this matter! And may the power of God be released into your ministry in Jesus' name!

The New Priesthood

Abraham paid tithe to Melchizedek.

> ***For this Melchizedek, king of Salem, priest of the Most High God, who met Abraham returning from the slaughter of the kings and blessed him, to whom also Abraham gave a tenth part of all, first being translated king of righteousness and then also king of Salem, meaning king of peace.***
> ***Heb. 7:1-2***

And it was commanded later that the sons of Levi should receive tithes from the people according to the Law.

> *And indeed those that are of the sons of Levi who receive the priesthood, have a commandment to receive tithes from the people according to the law.*
> *Heb. 7:5*

The priesthood of the order of Aaron was imperfect. But God has made provision for the coming of the Perfect One, Jesus Christ, according to the order of Melchizedek.

> *The Lord has sworn and will not relent, 'You are a priest forever according to the order of Melchizedek.'*
> *Psalm 110:4*

> *For the priesthood being changed, of necessity there is also a change of the law. Heb. 7:12*

As the priesthood is changed from the Levites to the believers, the law also changes from tithe to seed and the fellowship of ministering to the saints in liberty as practiced both by the Lord Jesus Christ and the early church.

> *and Joanna the wife of Chuza, Herod's steward, and Susanna, and many others who provided for Him (Jesus)* from their substance, Luke 8:3*

> *For on the one hand there is an annulling of the former commandment because of its weakness and unprofitableness, for the law made nothing perfect; on the other hand, there is the bringing in of a better hope, through which we draw near to God. Heb. 7:18-19*

The choice is really yours. You can either decide to obey or to disobey. As for the Bible it is unchanging. God has said it plainly here that he has annulled the former commandments. Do not forget that the subject of this passage is the old and new priesthood as they affect tithe. God has annulled the commandment of the tithe for the present dispensation, being a legalistic covenant, which is both weak and unprofitable to His purpose for the Church. It is the will of God to perfect the saint.

> *And He Himself gave some to be apostles, some prophets, some evangelists, and pastors and teachers, for the equipping of the saints for the work of ministry, for the edifying of the body of Christ, till we all come to the unity of the faith and the knowledge of the Son of God, to a perfect man, to the measure of the fullness of Christ.*
> *Eph. 4: 11-13*

And He knows that the law of the tithe cannot achieve this as it made nothing perfect. Therefore He nullified it. On the other hand, God has brought a better hope, which is Christ Jesus. Through this better hope, all that rightly apply it draw near to God. We shall see this better hope presently.

The high priests appointed by the law were imperfect men for they daily needed to offer sacrifices first for their own sins and then for the sins of the people. But our Lord Jesus Christ who is our High Priest (and we ourselves individual priests) has made one single sacrifice of His own blood that has been perfected forever.

> *He is holy, harmless, undefiled, separated from sinners and He is higher than the heavens. Heb. 7:26*

He is a worthy perfect High Priest and the new hope in the better covenant of today.

A new Covenant

> *For if that first covenant had been faultless, then no place would have been sought for a second. Because finding fault with them He says, 'Behold I will make a new covenant with the house of Israel and with the house of Judah…In that He says 'A new covenant,' He has made the first obsolete. Now what is become obsolete and growing old is ready to vanish away. Heb. 8: 7-13*

Like I said, the choice of obedience is yours. But know it right now that the old covenant under which the tithe operated has been made obsolete and you should allow it to vanish away. This is precisely why your faithfulness in tithes does not open the windows of heaven to the extent that was promised in the book of Malachi.

> *… and pour out such blessing that there will not be room enough to receive it.*
> *Mal. 3:10b*

The case of those who use tithe cards is even more pathetic. People are roped in by heresies and they obey the doctrines of men rather than the doctrines of Christ. They prefer to be led by the law rather than by the liberty of grace.

> *Knowing that a man is not justified by the works of the law but by faith in Jesus Christ, even we have believed in Christ Jesus, that we might be justified by faith in Christ and not by the works of the law; for by the works of the law no flesh shall be justified. Gal 2:16*

With the death of Christ, we entered into the new covenant in His blood. In this new covenant, justification does not come by the works of the law, such as the payment of tithes. Rather justification comes by faith in Christ. Righteousness does not come through the law, such as the tithe law, but by faith in Christ. If it were possible to achieve righteousness through the law, then there would have been no need for the Lord to die.

You have become estranged from Christ, you who attempt to be justified by law; you have fallen from grace. Gal. 5:4

The word is very explicit. Attempting to meet God's standard through the satisfaction of these legal ordinances such as the tithe, leads to estrangement from Christ and a fall from grace. If you get estranged from Christ, it means you are no longer a Christian. Again if you fall from grace, it also means you are no longer a Christian since we are saved by grace, Eph. 2:8. So make up your mind what to do. Either you go with the word of God or with the word and traditions of men. It is right and scripturally correct to say that those who live by the Mosaic Law, including the law of tithe, are no longer Christians. They are more of Judaists.

> *Why do your disciples transgress the tradition of the elders for they do not wash their hands when they eat bread? And He answered and said to them, 'And why do you yourselves transgress the commandment of God for the sake of your tradition? ... You hypocrites, rightly did Isaiah prophesy of you saying, 'This people honor Me with their lips, but their heart is far away from Me. But in vain do they worship Me, teaching as doctrines the precepts of men.' Matt. 15:2-9*

> *Neglecting the commandment of God, you hold to the tradition of men. Mark 7:8*

Many are unknowingly worshipping God in vain according to our Lord Jesus Christ. There is a need for you to read the Scriptures continuously in order to know the mind of God over certain issues. In the spiritual as well as in the material realm, ignorance is not an excuse in law. When you teach the precepts of men as the doctrines of God, your adherents will be misled into worshipping God in vain. How pathetic it is to realize that there are well-intended multitudes in this category, who are actually worshiping God in vain, wasting their resources in tithes. Do not forget that God values His word even above His name. His words will never change in sympathy for your errors. You must begin to read the Bible for yourself. Stop depending on the unverified teaching of men. They may just be wrong and misleading.

Collection for the Saints, 1Cor. 16:1-3

The early Church did not tithe. That was why there was a need for them to lay something aside to take care of the saints who were their spiritual leaders at Jerusalem.

> *Now concerning the collection for the saints, as I directed the churches of Galatia so do you also. On the first day of every week let each one of you put aside and save as he may prosper, that no collection be made when I come. 1Cor. 16:1-2 (NASB)*

The Geek word ***hagios*** translated as "saints" in the above passage refers to those who are separated, consecrated and devoted to the service of God. It refers to those whose work is the work of ministry. These people are supposed to be totally occupied with God's work. Paul the apostle, who was called, rejected the distractions of marriage and family life and chose to also have a secular job by which he provided for his own livelihood. This was his personal choice.

> *For you, yourselves know how you ought to follow us, for we were not disorderly among you; nor did we eat anyone's bread free of charge, but worked with labor and toil night and day, that we might not be a burden to any of you. 2Thess. 3:7-8*

In that his choice, Paul still recognized that there are still those involved in full-time ministry. The Churches made "Collection," not tithes, for Paul's team.

> *And when I arrive whomever you may approve, I shall send them with letters to carry your gifts to Jerusalem. 1Cor. 16:3 (NASB)*

The apostle did not approve of using the precious time of his ministry to be attending to collection of money and material. Rather this issue of providing for the need of the saints was to be attended to by each believer according to how he prospered. These believers were Spirit-led and so they were allowed to exercise their Christian liberty in determining what to lay aside for the saints. They discovered individually the benefits of giving bountifully.

The Fellowship of Ministering to the Saints

We read the testimony of Paul:

> ***For I bear witness that according to their ability, yes and beyond their ability they were freely giving, imploring us with much urgency that we would receive the gift and the fellowship of ministering to the saints. 2Cor. 8:3-4***

These believers actually gave beyond their ability and you can see that they gave so much that the apostles must have refused to accept that much. This made them to implore the apostles with much urgency to accept their gifts. How wonderful it would be if we follow the scriptural examples. This could not have been the tithe because the tithe was a specified proportion – ten percent. The people gave beyond their ability.

They gave out of love and not because they were persuaded by Paul. It is also interesting that these leaders recognized that what they gave were gifts. However, the believers were encouraged to abound in this grace of giving to the saints because of the blessings that accrue from it.

> *But as you abound in everything – in the faith, in speech, in knowledge, in diligence, and in your love for us – see that you abound in this grace also.*
> *2Cor. 8:7*

Apart from this giving of gifts to the saint at Jerusalem, they were also encouraged to give to one another to ensure equal care in the Body of Christ.

> *For I do not mean that others should be eased and you burdened; but by an*

> *equality, that now at this time, your abundance also may supply their lack that there may be equality.*
> *2Cor. 8:13-14*

The early church also provided for their ministers through the means of what was called 'the fellowship of ministering to the saints.' This is what Paul referred to in 1Cor. 16:1-2, when he ordered both the Galatians as well as the Corinthian churches to lay aside something, according to how they prospered. This gift, made as provision for their ministers, was to be made willingly.

> *Now concerning the ministering to the saints, it is superfluous for me to write to you; for I know your willingness, about which I boast of you to the Macedonians. And Achaia was ready a year ago; and your zeal has stirred up the majority, 2Cor. 9:1-2*

Their gifts were not to be offered as a grudging obligation (as you have most times in tithe today), but rather as a bountiful gift offered generously.

Therefore I thought it necessary to exhort the brethren to go to you ahead of time and prepare your bountiful gift beforehand, which you promised as a matter of generosity and not as a grudging obligation. But this I say: He who sows sparingly will also reap sparingly, and he who sows bountifully will also reap bountifully. So let each one give as he purposes in his heart, not grudgingly or of necessity; for God loves a cheerful giver, 2Cor. 9:5-7

Our seed should not just be the giving of God's portion while we have the rest. This was the error of Israel in the era of tithe that God complained about. Our seed ought to demonstrate to God that He has the ultimate place in our lives, from beginning to the end. See how the Israelite farmer waited for the ripening of his first fruit that he might bring it to the house of God, the Owner of the farm, the seed planted, and also the fruit harvested. God who searches the heart should see our willingness to give Him all. The Lord should not only have the first take but also the whole take in all our matters and interests, in all that we possess.

The Lord wants a people who will give Him their all, the Levites of the present day, who will be on the watch to bring God His right. When we become a people like that, we possess nothing that God may possess all things. The spiritual realities of this mindset drives God's kingdom like in the early apostolic era when men did not count their possessions as theirs but sold them and willingly surrendered the proceeds to the apostles. This should be the humble attitude with which we bring seed to God. It should always be God first, Matt. 22:36-38.

Another important aspect of the character of these believers of old was that they were careful to first give themselves to Jesus before giving their bountiful gifts.

> ***And this they did, not as we had hoped, but first gave themselves to the Lord and then to us by the will of God. 2Cor. 8:5***

Today, we see the reverse to be the case. Some preachers solicit for fraudsters and drug pushers to bring their money into their churches. They sometimes justify the source of their ill-gotten wealth to these despairing souls as a means of persuading them to give their money for the cause of their churches. The gospel of salvation becomes unmentionable to such people. Any preaching that would touch this sensitive area of fraud and sin is prohibited in these Churches. The devil has given the preachers of truth the tag of holiness preachers. Well, like it or not, Heb. 12:14 still holds true: without holiness no one can see the Lord.

> *For we are not like many, peddling the word of God, but as from sincerity but as from God, we speak in Christ, in the sight of God, 2Cor. 2:17 (NASB)*

The spiritual aspect of this new covenant source of providing for the leaders of our churches is shown in 2Cor. 9:10.

> *Now may He who supplies seed to the sower, and bread for food, supply and multiply the seed you have sown and increase the fruits of your righteousness. 2Cor. 9:10*

This means that God gives seed but you have to decide whether to eat it or to sow some. If you do sow some, then He will multiply and increase only what you have sown and it will be counted for you as a fruit of righteousness. The seed is your money or your resources. You sow it either by giving it to the saints or by applying it directly to the work of the gospel of Christ. When you do this willingly and cheerfully, unfailingly on the day of harvest you will reap a multiplied and bountiful reward. This is the spiritual method that God approves today for the church to care for their leaders.

> *Give and it will be given to you; good measure, pressed down, shaken together, and running over will be put into your bosom; for with the same measure that you use, it will be measured back to you. Luke 6: 38*

The thing is open. The measure that is the proportion that you sow, will determine the proportion that will be returned to you in harvest. Preach it in your churches and the Holy Spirit will touch your flock to bless you through this spiritual law of sowing and reaping. If you neglect it and you insist on operating by the old covenant tithe, you will have disappointments to contend with.

> *And I testify again to every man who becomes circumcised that he is a debtor to keep the whole law. You have become estranged from Christ you who attempt to be justified by law; you have fallen from grace. For we, through the Spirit, eagerly wait for the hope of righteousness by faith. Gal. 5:3-5*

The Purpose of the New Covenant

The purpose of this new covenant way is twofold. Firstly it supplies the need of the saints and secondly it makes the sower to abound with thanksgiving to God on his own day of harvest.

> *For the administration of this service not only supplies the need of the saints, but also is abounding through many thanksgiving to God. 2Cor. 9:12*

Obviously the sower will willingly sow a new and greater seed thereafter.

Another reason, I perceive, that recommends the use of this law of the Spirit of life is that those who are false leaders and false teachers will easily be recognized. The Spirit of God will never back them up. Whoever sows on them shall find them infertile. Prosperity of church leaders becomes directly tied to their spiritual prosperity. This is the will of God.

> ***Beloved, I pray that you may prosper in all things and be in health, just as your soul prospers. 3John 1:2***

The law of sowing and reaping is actually faith in action. Those who have no faith in God cannot operate it.

> ***For whatever is not from faith is sin. Rom. 14:23***

There is no need to solicit for people to sow on you as a leader. The church is commanded to do so according to what each one has, not according to what he does not have.

> ***For if the readiness is present, it is acceptable according to what a man***

has, not according to what he does not have. 2Cor. 8:12.

It is then in the place of the church leader who receives such gifts to pray to God, interceding for his flock out of a caring heart, that the Lord may meet their needs.

As a leader with the objective of fulfilling your ministry, your first priority should be to win and nurture souls unto maturity and to be able to present them to God. This you may not achieve if you begin by milking dry the new converts. Paul's conduct should be a good example to us.

But we were gentle among you, just as a nursing mother cherishes her own children. So affectionately longing for you, we were well pleased to impart to you, not only the gospel of God but also our own lives, because you had become dear to us. For you remember our labors and toil; for laboring night and day; that we might not be a burden to any of you. 1Thess. 2:1-9

Paul actually had to work to provide their own

personal needs in order not to burden those new converts. The gospel always took priority with them.

> *You are witnesses and God also how devoutly and justly and blamelessly we behaved our-selves among you who believe. 1Thess. 2:10*

This ought to be our example today. In the book of 1Corinthians chapter 9 the Lord gives the ministers of the gospel a right to reap the material things from their flock.

> *If we have sown spiritual things for you, is it a great thing if we reap your material things? 1Cor. 9:11*

> *Who plants a vineyard and does not eat of its fruit? Or who tends a flock and does not drink of the milk of the flock? 1Cor. 9:7*

Paul also wrote to the Galatians

> *And let the one who is taught the word share all good things with him who teaches. Do not be deceived; God is not*

mocked, for whatever a man sows, this he will reap. Gal. 6:6-7(NASB)

Therefore it is a God-given right that the leaders of the church should eat of the material and other resources of their followers. However, this must not be abused. It must be done according to the Spirit of life in Christ Jesus: sowing and reaping, not according to the obsolete law of tithe.

Instituted in Abraham

Even though tithe was instituted in Abraham and not in Moses, yet we must recognize that it became part of the legal requirements of the mosaic covenant.

> *And Melchizedek king of Salem brought out bread and wine, now he was a priest of God Most High, and He blessed him and said 'Blessed be Abram of God Most High, who has delivered your enemies into your hand.' And he gave a tenth of all. Gen. 14:18-20(NASB)*

At the end of every third year you shall bring out of the tithe of your produce in that year, and shall deposit it in your gates, and the Levite, because he has no portion or inheritance among you, and the alien, the orphan and the widow who are in your gates, shall come and eat and be satisfied, in order that the Lord your God may bless you in all the work of your hand which you do. Deut. 17:12 (NASB)

Was circumcision not given to Abraham long before Moses?

And every male among you who is eight days old shall be circumcised throughout your generation.
Gen. 17:12 (NASB)

Yet it formed part of the legal requirements of the Mosaic Law.

Speak to the sons of Israel, saying, When a woman gives birth and bears a male child, and on the eight day the flesh of his forsaken shall be circumcised. Lev. 12:2-3 (NASB.

When Christ came, was He not circumcised in that dispensation according to the law?

> *And when eight days were completed before His circumcision, His name was then called Jesus the name given by the angel before He was conceived in the womb. Luke 2:21 (NASB)*

Yet after the cross, any insistence on circumcision was viewed as an unnecessary encroachment on the believer's liberty and was totally condemned and rejected.

> *Behold I, Paul, say to you that if you receive circumcision, Christ will be of no benefit to you. And I testify again to every man who receives circumcision, that he is under obligation to keep the whole Law. You have been severed from Christ, you who are seeking to be justified by Law; you have fallen from grace. For we through the Spirit, by faith, are waiting for the hope of righteousness for in Christ Jesus neither circumcision nor un-circumcision means anything, but faith working through love.*

Gal. 5:2-6 (NASB)

Therefore, like circumcision even though it started in Abraham long before Moses, the tithe also formed part of the Law. Also like circumcision, the tithe was done away with in Christ as soon as He died on the cross.

In place of the legal imposition of the circumcision of the flesh is the spiritual requirement of the circumcision of the heart. This is the sanctification of the heart through the blood of Jesus.

> *But he is a Jew who is one inwardly, and circumcision is that which is of the heart, by the Spirit, not by the letter (the law); and his praise is not from men but from God. Rom. 2:29 (NASB)*

Those observances of the law all have spiritual significances today, in this our dispensation. Find out what they signify and you will know the mind of God for you today. This is one of the sources of false doctrine today. An example is the case of water baptism. When Jesus said in John 3:5 that you must be born of water to enter into the Kingdom of God, men decided that little children need to be baptized soon after birth in order for them not to miss heaven. This is the genesis of the error of infant baptism. But Jesus was not talking of physical water but rather of the water of the word of God, Eph. 5:25-27; Titus 3:5; 1Pet. 1:23; John 15:3.

And in Him you were also circumcised with the circumcision made without hands, in the removal of the body of the flesh by the circumcision of Christ. Col. 2:11 (NASB)

Similarly, in place of the legal imposition of the ten percent-tithe is the spiritual liberty of sowing and reaping as one purposes in his heart, knowing and recognizing the spiritual principal at work – whatever a man sows, that is what he shall reap. If you sow sparingly, you will reap sparingly. But if you sow bountifully, you will also reap bountifully. Thus the material prosperity of the believer lies in his own hands, to be received through a proper application of this spiritual law and not through prayer only. Prayer is the weeding and application of manure on the farmland in preparation for the sowing of your seed of righteousness. Despite the well-weeded farmland with manure properly applied, without sowing, there can be no harvest.

When we remove the legality of ten percent from it, the law is done away with and the liberty of the Holy Spirit is re-instituted. Therefore the law was teaching us, albeit by compulsion, the benefits of sowing, that of being a blessing, Gen. 12:12. But now that the law is fulfilled in Christ, all the righteous requirement of the law must be fulfilled (retained) in us who are spiritual, Rom. 8:4. The righteous requirement of the law in this case is that we reap whatever we sow. Christians today wallow in poverty and bring reproaches to God's kingdom because they have let the word of God work against them.

They thus perish in ignorance. In the name of Christian liberty they fail to sow and yet expect to reap simply because they prayed to God. Incidentally, the word of God cannot fall to the ground void.

> *For as the rain and the snow come down from heaven, and do not return there without watering the earth, and*

> *making it bear and sprout, and furnishing seed to the sower and bread to the eater; so shall My word be which goes forth from My mouth. It shall not return to Me empty without accomplishing what I desire and without succeeding in the matter for which I sent it, Isaiah 55:10-11 (NASB)*

When you hear that we are no longer under the law, it does not mean that we are now lawless. The law in this case being referred to is the mosaic law of sin and death. But we are definitely under the law of the Spirit of life in Christ Jesus.

> *For the law of the Spirit of life in Christ Jesus has set me free from the law of sin and of death. Rom. 8:2 (NASB)*

This law of the Spirit of life in Christ Jesus is written in our hearts. The Holy Spirit in us confirms this law. Even as you are reading the word of God in the Bible, He is confirming it and refuting any falsehood taught you by any man.

For this is the covenant that I will make with the house of Israel after those days, says the Lord; I will put my laws into their minds, and I will write them upon their hearts; and I will be their God and they shall be My people. Heb. 8:10 (NASB)

Nothing to Sow

Some may argue that they are so poor that they have nothing to sow. Remember Isaac who was caught up with famine and his livelihood was so threatened that he wanted to run away to Egypt. But God forbade this, promising to bless him in the land of famine, Gen. 26:1-6, and 12. Note however that despite the promise of the Most High to bless Isaac in Gerar, in the land where there was a famine, God still required the man to first sow before he would expect to reap the promised blessing.

Sojourn in this land and I will be with you and bless you, for to you and to your descendants I will give all these lands, and I will establish that oath which I swore to your father Abraham.

And I will multiple your descendants as the stars of heaven and will give your descendants all these lands; and by your descendants all the nations of the earth shall be blessed, Gen. 26:3-4 (NASB)

Now Isaac sowed in that land and reaped in the same year a hundredfold. And the Lord blessed him and the man became rich and continued to grow richer until he became very wealthy; for he had possessions of flocks and herds and a great household so that the Philistines envied him. Gen. 26:12-14 (NASB)

Settle it therefore in your heart that you must sow in order to reap. Faith without works is useless. No amount of fasting and prayer can bring in the expected blessing if you do not add the spiritual work element of sowing. Many have also assumed that when James was writing about the work element of faith, he was writing exclusively about your labor input. No! In actual fact what James was referring to as work in James 2:14-26, is the seed of being a blessing to others, which you sow.

> *What use is it my brethren if a man says he has faith but he has no works? Can that faith save him? If a brother or sister is without clothing and in need of daily food, and one of you says to them, 'Go in peace, be warmed and be filled.' And you do not give them what is necessary for their body, what use is that? Even so faith if it has no works, is dead being by itself.*
> *James 2:14-17 (NASB)*

So we are expected to do good, to give and to sow in order that we may be materially blessed.

> *And let us not lose heart in doing good, for in due time we shall reap if we do not grow weary. So then, while we have opportunity let us do good to all men and especially to those who are of the household of the faith.*
> *Gal. 6:9-10 (NASB)*

In Isaiah 55:10 God promised that He would furnish us with the seed we need to sow.

And furnishing seed to the sower and bread to the eater. Isaiah 55:10

It is however left to you to decide whether you will eat all your seed or your will sow some and eat others.

Now He, who supplies seed to the sower and bread for food, will supply and multiply your seed for sowing and increase the harvest of your righteousness. 2Cor. 9:10 (NASB)

Although God supplies both your seed to be sown as well as the bread of your food, He will only multiply the seed that you have sown, your acts of righteous giving. God does not multiply the bread you eat. He only supplies it. But if you want to live in the realm of multiplicity of blessings, then you must sow seeds of righteousness. If you eat all your seed, do not expect multiplied blessings, for wealth comes only to those who will sow seed and be a blessing to other people.

Therefore do not be anxious. God has promised that He will provide the initial seed that you are to sow. That seed may be very small initially but you are not to despise it.

> ***Though your beginning was insignificant yet your end will increase greatly. Job 8:7 (NASB)***

Start with whatever you have. Use it to bless someone else. Sow on your day of famine and God will not lightly esteem your seed. The tougher it is to sow, the higher the sacrifice will be regarded and so the greater your harvest shall be. Follow the Holy Spirit in this new covenant law of sowing and reaping and the Lord will greatly bless both you and your flock in Jesus name, Amen!

Understanding the Role of Prophecy

Many erroneously assume that as soon as the promise of God is secured in any matter, then its actualization is at the exclusion of their own role. The promise of God gives you the seed to sow. It never gives you a straight harvest. It only provides your seed. It provided the seed for Isaac to sow in order to receive the harvest promised by God. Isaac could never have received the promises of God until he sowed.

You must move forward and sow if you are to actualize that dream of yours in Christ Jesus. Without the sowing of seed, there can be no harvest.

> *For as the rain cometh down, and the snow from heaven, and returneth not thither, but watereth the earth, and maketh it bring forth and bud, that it may give seed to the sower, and bread to the eater; so shall My word be that goeth forth out of My mouth; it shall not return unto Me void, but it shall accomplish that which I please, and it shall prosper in the thing whereto I sent it. Isaiah 55:10-11 (KJV)*

When one sows a seed, it does not immediately begin to produce a harvest of fruits. There is usually a gestation period determined by the type of seed sown and also by the mysteries of God. God only knows the right gestation period for each seed we sow. It is instructive that maize seed is harvested after just three months gestation. But it is harvested just once. Mango seed and orange seed will need at least three years gestation (that is for the improved breed) before there can be a harvest. But once you patiently wait that long and begin to harvest, you will be harvesting it every year. It thus appears that those seeds that require longer gestation periods provide us with greater harvests. Similarly, those prayers that appear to take longer to receive their answers provide us with greater blessings when the answers do come.

God is so good that He makes provision for our upkeep during the time that we are waiting for the gestation of our sown seed. The promise is that His word of promise will give us both the seed to sow as well as the bread that will sustain us during the gestation period, during the time that we wait for the answered prayers. Praise God!

True Freedom

The day you were born again, the Lord made you free. That freedom becomes real in each instance of truth that you get to know through the word of God.

> ***And you shall know the truth, and the truth shall make you free. John 8:32***

This freedom must not be viewed lightly because it took the life of our Lord Jesus Christ to secure it.

> ***Stand fast therefore in the liberty by which Christ has made us free, and do not be entangled again with a yoke of bondage. Gal. 5:1***

Also Apostle Paul further writes:

> ***You have become estranged from Christ you who attempt to be justified by law. Gal. 5:4***

> ***I do not set aside the grace of God for if righteousness comes through the law then Christ died in vain. Gal 2:21***

You have to make up your mind whom to follow, Christ or man. In these passages, the law referred to is the law of sin and of death. However, the law of the Spirit of life in Christ Jesus, under which every Spirit-led believer operates, is written in our hearts. That is why are called to give for the fellowship of ministering to the saints "as a man purposes in his heart."

Let each one do just as he has purposed in his heart; not grudgingly or under compulsion; for God loves a cheerful giver. 2Cor. 9:7

The kind of heart referred to is a heart under the control of the Holy Spirit. Follow the Holy Spirit as He leads you and do not harden your hearts because of immediate benefits. Have faith that the hearts of all men are in God's hands to control however He wills, Proverbs 21:1.

He will never disappoint you whenever you obey Him whether as a giver or as a receiver. For you as a giver, when your leader is ministering spiritual things to you and you are prospering thereby, know that he has a God-given right to partake of those your material benefits. As you walk together thus, love is promoted and grumbling and murmuring are eliminated from the church. Reproaches will give way to the glorification of our God in Jesus' name, Amen.

The Righteous Requirements of the Law, Rom. 8:4

> *What shall say then? Is the law sin? May it never be! So then the law is holy and the commandment is holy and righteous and good, Rom 7:7, 12 (NASB)*

> *But before faith came, we were kept in custody under the law, shut up to the faith, which was later to be revealed. Therefore the law has become our tutor to lead us to Christ, that we may be justified by faith. But now that faith has come we are no longer under a tutor. Gal. 3:23-25*

Actually the law showed us what we needed to achieve. But now righteousness, which could not be achieved by the law, is achieved by faith in Christ. Even though we are not under the law, as many of us as are led by the Spirit of God must have the righteous requirements of the law fulfilled in us. Therefore God used tithe, one tenth of our income, to teach us that there is a portion of our income that we ought to sow. Led by the Holy Spirit, in liberty you will minister the seed of your income to the gospel work.

In my experience, I hardly know of any believer that is walking in the spirit that still sows only one tenth. Almost always the testimony is that the love of God leads us to sow more than a tenth of our income. The Spirit retains this liberty. You are free to sow either more or less than ten percent of your income. Only recognize the spiritual law at work. If you sow more, you will reap more but if you sow less, you should also expect to reap less irrespective of your fasting and prayer.

> ***But if you are led by the Spirit, you are not under the law. Gal. 5:18 (NSAB)***

The law of the Spirit of life in Christ Jesus encourages you not to sow less but rather to sow much more than tithe and consequently to reap more abundantly, Matt. 5:20.

> ***...I came that they might have life and might have it abundantly, John 10:10 (NASB)***

> ***Now the Lord is the Spirit; and where the Spirit of the Lord is, there is liberty. 2Cor. 3:17 (NASB)***

It is not during service that you decide what to sow. You are supposed to lay it aside and to save it, at the time that the profit is made. You should bring the seed to sow in the very next service after it becomes available to you. If you have regard for your circumstances, you may never be able to sow. Sow it as soon as you have it available, not looking at outward circumstance. Do not delay it.

> *When you make a vow to God, do not be late in paying it, for He takes no delight in fools. Pay what you vow! Eccl. 5: 4 (NASB)*

The Holy Spirit cannot lead you not to sow after you have prospered. That would be contrary to God's word and He does not operate contrary to the word of the Bible. On the other hand He cannot lead you to sow what you do not have but what you do have.

> *For if the readiness is present it is acceptable according to what a man has, not according to what he does not have. 2Cor. 8:12 (NASB)*

You can determine to sow fifteen, twenty percent or even a greater proportion. But whatever you have covenanted with God, do not fail, but be ever faithful. You can also seek God's will to determine what to sow each time you need to sow. You should enjoy your liberty in Christ knowing the spiritual laws that guide your liberty – whosoever sows sparingly, shall of the same reap sparingly. And whosoever sows bountifully, shall also reap bountifully. A believer retains the freedom of sowing according to how he purposes in his heart at each instance of his seed sowing. He always reserves the right to increase or reduce his seed to be sown. But he must remember that whatever he sows that is what he should expect to reap, either sparingly or bountifully, according to his own choice of seed made in liberty of the spirit. Each time you sow, you perform an act of faith which pleases God, Heb. 11:6.

Tithe means the tenth. The point is that the Spirit of God does not restrict you to one tenth. And anything outside of the one tenth is no longer tithe. Most believers sow more than one tenth. These will discover that they are already practicing what I teach you. Again, one can decide to sow all that he has. He can even refuse to sow anything at all. He is a free moral agent. But let him not expect to reap where he did not sow, 2Cor. 9:6 and Gal. 6:7. Now, the purpose of the believer's heart is according to the directives of the Holy Spirit. That is why he did not consider one tenth sufficient in his heart.

Whatever you sow different from one tenth - either smaller or bigger - is no longer a tithe. Tithe simply means one tenth. So do not walk into the error of assuming that the Christian Liberty is to relieve you from investing in the work of God. Rather, it teaches you to invest much more in order that you may reap abundance. Who has ever harvested where he sowed nothing?

> *Do not be deceived, God is not mocked for whatever a man sows, this he will also reap. Gal. 6:7 (NASB)*

We conclude with the words of Charles F. Baker

The Israelites were subjected to a ten percent income tax, better known as the law of the tithe. Believers in this present Dispensation are not under the law, but it is generally conceded that if the law required one–tenth of ones income, the believer under grace should be constrained by the love of Christ to give at least that much or more. Paul does not lay down any percentage. He simply states that sparse sowing will result in a sparse harvest and that every man should give 'as he purposeth in his heart...not grudgingly or of necessity: for God loveth a cheerful giver.' 'Some have been entrusted with very little of this world's goods, but if there be first a willing mind, it is accepted according to that a man hath, and not according to that he hath not.' A Dispensational Theology by Charles F. Baker (Second Edition Pg.631).

CHAPTER SIX

WHO IS EXALTED, YOU OR GOD?

The attitude of receiving glory for miracles performed by God is an insult on God. When miracles take place, it is because God wills them to happen. Without Him we are totally powerless and can do nothing.

> ***...without Me you can do nothing.***
> ***John 15:5***

Even though we believe that God answers our prayers, yet each time He does so, especially when great miracles and wonders are manifested we cannot help but we surprised at the great power of our God. Unfortunately many of those who are so mightily used by God to perform such miracles soon fall into the error of arrogating the power of God's miracles to themselves. Soon enough the devil deceives them into thinking that the power came as a result of their personal holiness or prayer ability.

> ***But when Peter saw this, he replied to the people, Men of Israel, why do you gaze at us, as if by our own power or piety we had made him walk…***
> ***Act. 3:12***

It is a great evil before God to take His glory. Our God is a very jealous God when it comes to sharing His glory with man. As a result of this attitude, many have lost great budding ministries. When you assume that it is by your power, God soon withdraws His power from you and you are left empty but with a great followership who all have expectations that God will reach and bless them through you. Some have fallen into the devil's trap in this manner. When the power is gone due to the sin of self-glorification and pride, they go to the devil to obtain alternative power. Believe me such leaders have no obligation to preach the true gospel of Jesus Christ. Their master is the devil and it is his dictates that they follow.

It is through such fallen preachers that we hear heresies and demonic doctrines, which emanate with subtlety from their master the devil. Many who chase after signs and wonders fall into the hands of these fallen preachers. Therefore, instead of manifesting great healing powers that will benefit mankind, they would rather just use their powers to push people down in demonstration that they are powerful men of God. But who is powerful, you or God?

These men will invariably rule their flock with the vicious instrument of fear. They will teach you that if you leave their churches, you are doomed. But let me ask you. Is the church theirs or does it belong to Jesus Christ who also owns all the other true churches? If the true churches all belong to Jesus, why would you be doomed if you leave one and go to another church of Jesus Christ? If you fear them, they have got you! But if you show faith in Christ and refuse to be held under their bondage, then that Christ who is in you will prevail over them, Matt. 16:18, 1John 4: 4.

Returning God's Glory

It is only natural that when God has used you to do great exploits men will tend to glorify you instead of God. This is because you are their point of physical contact with God. They cannot see God but they see you. It is however in your place, as one that has superior knowledge of the ways of God, to warn them not to fall into this error. God expects that you will direct glory, honor, worship and thanksgiving to Him. But if you take His place and stand as the mighty miracle worker for the sake of material benefits, one day He will leave you and you will be stripped of all your spiritual power and anointing. Where then will you be?

Always return God's glory to Him. He has no need for material thanksgiving. If that comes, it is for you. But He is pleased when His name, not yours, is glorified. Even in the church, advertise Jesus, not yourself. There is no benefit (except of course to you) in introducing you with a citation of your previous spiritual exploits when you are coming to preach the word of God. It definitely does not build up the faith of your audience. Rather it may antagonize you with the spiritually enlightened ones among them. Who are you to take God's glory without fear? Be warned that men of old that tried it were cut down to size and if you continue thus, soon enough He will cut you down to size too, Isaiah 42:8, Heb. 12:29, Prov. 29:1.

Have you not heard that if you humble yourself before Him, He will lift you up? But if lift yourself up in pride, He will resist you and humble you.

> ***Humble yourself in the presence of the Lord, and He will exult you.***
> ***James 4:10 (NASB)***
>
> ***So that he sets on high those who are lowly, and those who mourn are lifted to safety, Job 5:11(NASB)***
>
> ***Thus says the Lord God…exalt that which is low and abase that which is high, Ezekiel 21:269 (NASB).***

He has brought down rulers from their thrones. And has exalted those who were humble, Luke 1:52 (NASB)

But He gives greater grace. Therefore it says, 'God is opposed to the proud, but gives grace to the humble.' James 4:6 (NASB)

Are you called powerful? Please tell them it is God who is powerful and not you. He alone is the Omnipotent One, the Alfa and the Omega, the Lord of Hosts, the Creator of all things; He that says, "Yes" and none can reverse it, He whose counsel only shall stand. *Father, to You is the glory forever and ever, Amen!*

What Is Your Commission?

Every man called by God has a commission. There is a definite thing that God has called you to do for the furtherance of His Kingdom. You must go back to your commission if you have left it to go for what seems fashionable and in vogue. If God has called you as an evangelist and you go to found a church just because it is now the lucrative thing to do in ministry, your ministry is yet unfulfilled and you can never excel. Return to your commission. It is not the purpose of God in calling you simply to enrich you. Yes, riches are our heritage but the purpose of our calling must be the very breath of life to us.

> *But you be sober in all things, endure hardship, do the work of an evangelist, fulfill your ministry, 2Tim. 4:5 (NASB)*

God does not expect to receive excuses from you. He found you worthy and so He called you. If your ministry appears hard, do not avoid what God expects you to endure. Many Christians fail at this point. It is the mark of a good soldier of the cross when you suffer for the sake of the Gospel.

> *Suffer hardship with me, as a good soldier of Christ Jesus. 2Tim. 2:3 (NASB)*

> *Therefore do not be ashamed of the testimony of our Lord, or of me His prisoner; but join with me in suffering for the gospel according to the power of God, 2Tim 1:8 (NASB)*

It is not every minister whose ministry will bring him riches. Ministry is not like a vocation of personal choice. Therefore your success is not measured on the same yardstick as that of the secular world. Look, you are not called to satisfy the expectations of any man or to please men.

> ***For am I now seeking the favor of men, or of God? Or am I striving to please men? If I were still trying to please men, I would not be a bond-servant of Christ. For I would have you know, brethren, that the gospel, which was preached by me, is not according to man, nor was I taught it but I received it through a revelation of Jesus Christ, Gal. 1:10-12***

How did you receive your calling? Was it from man of from Christ? The Lord Jesus Christ never attempted to please any man during His earthly ministry.

> ***But Jesus, on His part, was not entrusting Himself to them, for He knew all men, and because He did not***

need anyone to bear witness concerning man, for He himself knew what was in man, John 2:24-25 (NASB)

You are called to please only God. Fulfill your ministry. Know precisely what God has commissioned you to do and do it with all your heart. In achieving this you may not be rich but you will be fulfilled. The Lord has also promised to care for you. Just fulfill your ministry and you would have satisfied the reason for your existence. How many of the notable ministers of past ages were rich men. Many, who were rich when called, invested all their riches into the gospel and died as fulfilled men, even if not as rich men. Fulfill your ministry!

God did not call you and anoint you with His power just for your self-glorification. When you have made yourself a wolf before your flock and they live in dread of your God-given power, Jesus is no longer glorified. He does not rule His people by the use of raw force but rather by the refined irresistible force of love. He desires that His people be liberated from the bondage of the enemy, Satan.

So, why do you now use His power to bind His people, putting them under your slavery? No, He may take back His Spirit and His power and leave you empty.

> *And where the Spirit of the Lord is there is liberty, 2Cor. 3:17 (NASB)*

Our Prayer Lives

When you rule God's people as a tyrant, you will not have the boldness to stand before God without condemnation. The result is that you will spend very little time in prayer, and your prayers shall be nothing short of a list of petitions. How can you enjoy the rich fellowship of simply being in the presence of the Lord and basking in His love and glory if you are too busy planning the latest tricks to use to bind His people further to yourself, receiving His glory? You cannot be stealing from God and expect to have deep loving fellowship with Him.

Some of these people have even begun to condemn the spiritual principles of fasting and preaching its de – merits. There is great joy in having fellowship with the Holy One. That is what Paul meant when he said:

> *For the kingdom of God is not food and drink but righteousness and peace and joy in the Holy Spirit. Rom 14:17 (NASB)*

The kingdom of God is not in the amount of money and material you can acquire from the church for the satisfaction of your covetous appetite. The testimony of the faith of many is solely based on the material miracles that they have received from God. You can be blessed with a lot of miracles and you still go to hell, Matt. 7:21-23. Therefore, do not let your Christianity be assessed on the basis of the amount of miracles you have received. There is great joy in having fellowship with God's Spirit. When you have tasted Him, you will come to know that truly God is good!

The Body of Christ

The church belongs to no man. Even if you are the founder of a local church, you are only a part of the Body of Christ. The church is the Body of Christ and God has apportioned various responsibilities to various people in the church. It is just incidental that God gave you the responsibility of organizing the church into existence in your locality. You should simply perform your assigned task, fulfilling your ministry and let God have His glory. So the claim by some ministers of God that the church is theirs is nothing but a display of spiritual ignorance, ignorance of God's purpose in setting up their local churches. God can ask you to leave the work in the hands of another soon after properly setting up the church.

God intends to use each local church to reach the unreached. If you allow this universal vision of Jesus to die, then surely you are not fulfilling your ministry.

Occupy till I come, Luke 19:13(KJV)

God's heartbeat is the salvation of souls not the enrichment of His ministers. Your enrichment is nothing but an addition and not the objective.

> *But seek first the kingdom and His righteousness and all these things shall*

be added to you, Matt. 6:33 (NASB)

Do not let the church resources that should be purposefully invested in the spread of the gospel find their way into your pockets. And when the need of the gospel arises, the church would only discover that their pastor has depleted the church coffers for the provision of his personal luxuries. One day, you will give an account to the Lord who owns the Church for every kobo. Unless you repent and desist from such ways, you will not be found guiltless.

CHAPTER SEVEN

PROPHETIC DECEPTION

Today, prophecy has been given undue emphasis in our churches. Probably due to the hard economic times, people tend to seek for relief from their material needs as a priority. Spiritual prosperity appears to have taken the backbench in our churches. Any preaching of the gospel that fails to address the issues of the belly is not a good message. But whenever a message touches this sensitive area, everybody appears to come alive with the resounding echo of agreement, "AMEN!" Many appear to have forgotten the warning of Scriptures concerning prophetic deception especially in these last days.

> ***Beware of false prophets who come to you in sheep's clothing, but inwardly are ravenous wolves.***
> ***Matt. 7:15 (NASB)***

You are warned to beware of them. The Lord says that they will not come looking like they are wolves but rather they will come in the garb of the sheep. So if you think that the Lord is referring to those obvious white garment juju priests, you are mistaken. He says that they will come in sheep's clothing. Look for them behind your Pentecostal pulpits.

They have already infiltrated. Their motives will not be obvious but cunningly hidden, like their master the devil taught them. The Lord reveals that although they look like the sheep, inwardly in the intents of their hearts is hidden the singular objective of devouring the sheep. When a wolf hides among the sheep, what has he in mind except to devour the sheep? When a cat hides among rats what other hidden agenda has he except to devour the unsuspecting rats? In the same manner they have nothing else in mind expect to destroy your Christian faith.

Like their master did to Eve, they are seeking for opportunities to deceive you through distorting the word of truth. They will carefully sneak in heresies and falsehood in order to deceive those who are unstable. Periodically they will be introducing new doctrines, claiming that it is not everything that the Lord taught that is written down in Scriptures. Thus they strive to sustain their false doctrine by claims of special revelations.

> *And there are also many other things which Jesus did, which if they were written in detail, I suppose that even the world itself would not contain the books, which were written. John 21:25 (NASB)*

They however forget that it is the Lord that caused to be written those things that were written, for our own learning. Also the Lord ensured that what is written is complete and adequate to equip us.

All Scripture is inspired by God and profitable for teaching, for reproof, for training in righteousness that the man of God may be adequate; thoroughly equipped for every good work. 2Tim. 3:16-17(NASB)

The warning against these false prophets is a major issue with the Lord.

And many false prophets will arise, and will mislead many, Matt. 24: 11

The Lord warns that the number of false prophets that will arise will be numerous. Is this prophecy not being fulfilled in our generation? Christians now seek after prophecy.

Any service without a word of prophecy sounding forth is interpreted as silence from heaven, even though there has been a great expository teaching of the Bible in that service. Some weak leaders have allowed their flock to rule them by submitting to their incessant request for prophecy, signs and wonders. My friend, rise up to your responsibility and shepherd the flock of thee

Lord. They are sheep that can easily go astray. That is why the Lord has made you an overseer among them. You have an account to render to He that called you. Therefore do not let the sheep lead you but rather shepherd the flock of God.

Be careful whom you give your pulpits to. The wolves are out there seeking opportunities to destroy the flock of God in your charge. Be careful my brother. Jesus says that these many false prophets will mislead many. Therefore an action does not become right just because the majority of pastors practice it. Some of those practices you see on foreign gospel video films are the activities of false prophets. Follow the word, follow Jesus and do not follow men.

> ***Fixing our eyes on Jesus the author and perfecter of faith.***
> ***Heb. 12:1(NASB)***

Do not ever follow the crowd. Two thousand years ago, the Lord warned us to enter by the small gate and the narrow way that are found by a few. The wide gate and that broad way, lead only to destruction.

Enter by the narrow gate; for the gate is wide, and the way is broad that leads to destruction and many are those who enter by it. For the gate is small, and the way is narrow that leads to life and few are those who find it. Matt. 7:13-14(NASB)

Money, money, money, that is all that virtually all the people are after in the churches. Do you think that Jesus has changed? When He gave the five thousand people free food, the next day they surged again expecting a similar performance. But the Lord did not allow the crowd to change His ministry to become the ministry of bread and fish. He rather advised them to seek for the food that is eternal, John 6:22-25, John 6:26-27.

Those multitudes were seeking Jesus, not because they saw signs of His life-changing ministry, not because they saw signs of everlasting joy and peace, but because Jesus provided them with loaves, which they ate and were filled. How many in your church today are seeking Jesus for eternal life's sake and how many are seeking Him for the loaves. Instead of obliging them with fresh signs and wonders, the Lord preached to them on the benefits of eating His flesh and drinking His blood. He extolled the eternal qualities of taking in the word of God, John 6:50-51, 53. Can you speak the same message to your flock, Deut. 8:3?

Jesus boldly spoke this message to His flock not desiring to have a large followership made up of unbelieving disciples but rather desiring to pose a challenge that will eliminate the unserious bread seekers. He removed their focus from the physical food and set it on the spiritual food without which, He said, they would have no life in themselves.

> *Do not lay up for yourselves treasures upon the earth, where moth and rust destroy, and where thieves break in and steal. But lay up for yourselves treasures in heaven where neither moth nor rust destroys, and where thieves do not break in or steal; for where your treasure is, there will your heart be also, Matt. 6:19-21 (NASB)*

My friend, unless you lay up heavenly

treasures for yourself you are a loser in the final analysis.

> *If then you have been raised up with Christ keep seeking the things above where Christ is, seated at the right hand of God. Set your mind on the things above, not the things that are on the earth, Col. 3: 1-2 (NASB)*

Many today are born again yet all their attention is set on the things that are on the earth. Many have no eternal or heavenly vision. The coming of the Lord, to them, sounds like a myth, yet they are called believers. As a believer, you are seated at the right hand of God where Christ is. When He was enthroned, you were enthroned together with Him. And there is overwhelming evidence that heavenly things are more important and more exciting than earthly things. In an attempt to correct the imbalance that overemphasized spiritual things to the total exclusion of things needed for life here on earth, Christians are now guilty of overreaction. The full gospel has to have a place for material prosperity. But when this happens at the exclusion of true Christian virtues, that becomes the path of destruction. If you follow the spiritual principles of sowing and reaping as outlined earlier, you will prosper materially. But do not let this take the place of your spiritual well being, John 6:54-58.

He did not oblige them with another miracle of loaves and fishes. Rather He used the previously performed miracle as a channel to send forth the message that brought Him to this world. As a result of this hard preaching, many of His disciples stopped following Him. The weed, through the word, was separated from the wheat, John 6:66-69.

When you teach them the truth, as you ought to, your congregation must thin down. The miracle seekers will find their way out of the church. When the Lord preached it, it was not some but many of his disciples who withdrew. But note that the few that stayed back caught the vision of eternal life. Peter replied Him, "You have the word of eternal life." What kind of word do you feed your congregation with? In fact, I dare ask you: what kind of word do you have? Do you have words of bread and butter only? Are you involved in winning and maturing souls for Christ or are you in ministry to make millionaires out of people?

The Identification Mark of Falsehood

I thank God because He gave us the Bible to reveal the hidden things. As a loving Father, God did not leave us at the mercy of these false prophets. He gave a sign by which we can identify them.

> ***You will know them by their fruit. Grapes are not gathered from thorn brushes, nor figs from thistles, are they? An evil tree bears bad fruit. A good tree cannot produce bad fruit nor can a bad tree produce good fruit.***
> ***Matt. 7:16-18***

A false prophet is a bad tree. Jesus says that he cannot produce good fruit. The fruit is the character, the life of the prophet.

> ***Therefore if any man is in Christ, he is a new creature; the old things passed away; behold, new things have come.***
> ***2Cor. 5:17***

Unless that heart is regenerated, it cannot produce good fruit. When Jesus is not in the man, it is Satan that motivates his prophecies. That is why he sometimes attains a very high level of accuracy. He is nothing but a fortune-teller. God has a different focus. He is not immediately out to bless you materially. If God does it with your spiritual life yet unchanged, the blessing will destroy you.

> ***But the God of all grace, who hath called us unto His eternal glory by Christ Jesus, after that ye have suffered a while, make you perfect, stablish, strengthen, settle you. 1Peter 5:10 (KJV)***

The seven-year old pilot Jessica Dubroff was probably killed because she was too young to pilot an aircraft. If you let your twelve-year old son have your car keys because you love him and cannot refuse him, you may just succeed in destroying His life and thus you lose Him permanently. God does not want to lose you; therefore despite His great love for you, He would like you to first be mature enough to handle His blessings, lest those very blessings destroy your spiritual progress and life. Therefore in His infinite love, He has instituted his priorities.

> *For all these things the Gentiles eagerly seek; for your heavenly Father knows that you need all these things. But seek first His kingdom and His righteousness and all these things shall be added unto you.*
> *Matt. 6:32-33 (NASB)*

God has priorities. The things to seek are His kingdom and His righteousness. When you find these, He will give you the material blessings as addition. They are really not the substance. The substance is eternal life and the righteousness that comes through faith in Christ.

Therefore the false prophet will be manifesting evil fruit. When a prophet has more than one wife, it is an indication that he is a false prophet.

> *An overseer then must be above reproach the husband of one wife, temperate, hospitable, able to teach, not*

> *addicted to wine or pugnacious but gentle, un-contentious free from the love of money, 1 Tim. 3:2-3*

When the prophet is given to wine, he is a false prophet. When the prophet loves money, he is a false prophet. When he is violent, and rough, contentious and unyielding, it is a sure mark of his falsehood. In short if the prophet does not have the fruit of the Holy Spirit, then he is false.

> *But the fruit of the Spirit is love, joy, peace, patience, kindness, goodness, faithfulness, gentleness, self-control; against such things there is no law." Gal. 5:22-23*

You will know them by their fruit. By the word of Scriptures identify whether your prophet is true or false.

Accuracy of Prophecy

The devil has deceived many by this means. As was earlier said, the accuracy of prophecy does not authenticate its divine origin. The devil as a spirit has ability to see things that are invisible with the human eyes. He therefore can make deductions and predication that could be right on target, bull's eye. Also spirits can see your spiritual garments and marks. If the blood of Jesus is on the lintels of the doorpost of your heart, the devil knows it. If not, he also knows it. When your spiritual garment is dirty and filthy due to self-righteousness, he knows it. When your garment is full of violence due to immorality and cheating of your marriage partner (Mal. 2:14-16), he knows it. From these, Satan can deceive you with false prophecy. But look for the quality of life of the prophet and not on the accuracy of his prophecy because a good tree cannot bear bad fruit.

Purpose of Prophecy

If prophecy does not do any one of these things, it is false.

> *But one who prophesies speaks to men for edification, exhortation and consolation, 1 Cor. 14:2*

If the prophecy does not build you up, encourage you or comfort you, then it is not of

God. God does not send prophets of doom. If calamity is coming as a result of sin and God desires to warn you by prophecy, it will be a conditional prophecy. There will always be a chance given for repentance. That was how Nineveh was saved after Jonah prophesied against it. They repented and God relented. Also there is no true prophecy that can be contrary to the written word of God. All prophecies must agree with the written revelation of the Bible. Whenever a prophet claims ability to perform miracles, whether you believe it or not, it is a mark that he is false. When Jesus went to Nazareth, His hometown, to preach, they were so familiar with Him that they could not exercise faith in Him. Because of their unbelief; he could not do many miracles there, Matt. 13:53; Mark 6:1-6.

And he could do no miracle there except that He laid His hands upon a few sick people and healed them. And he wondered at their unbelief, Mark 6:5-6

If Jesus could not perform miracles because of the people's unbelief, how can a man today, in the name of a prophet, claim that he will perform miracles, whether you believe it or not? That is a sign that his power is not from God and is therefore devilish, Rom. 14:23. The man is a magician. Beware! Whatever he gives you, he will receive something greater from you in return. They will tell you "seeing is believing." But my Bible says that we walk by faith not by sight, 2Cor. 5:7

Instead of chasing signs and wonders, why don't you let signs and wonders follow you.

> ***And these signs will follow those that believe… Mark 16:17.***

What you seek for, the Lord will perform in His due time. But He can never change His sovereign word because you are of the opinion that God should do it now. His will is that you must first of all seek His kingdom and His righteousness. Without these tickets, you can never get the abundant material blessings you seek from the Lord. And since the Lord has made an investment in you with the blood of His Son Jesus Christ, you will not even get these material things if you go seeking them from the devil. You may get killed in the process because that is what the devil is really after.

Do not be afraid of the devil or his false prophets. Repent and renounce them. God will deliver you from your fears, troubles and burdens.

> ***I sought the Lord and He answered me, and delivered me from all my fears… this poor man cried and the Lord heard him and saved him out of all his troubles. The angel of the Lord encamps around those who fear Him and rescues them, Psalm 34:4-7 (NASB)***

There is an anointing in this message that if you covenant with God to reject Satan, surrender his charms which his agents gave you, renounce his works now, and confess your acceptance that Jesus is your Savior and Lord, no satanic repercussion can ever hurt you (Luke 10:19). And as long as you remain true to this covenant, that burden which took you to Satan in the first place, shall be removed in God's due time and you will never see it again in Jesus name.

Do not fear! Take your stand and see the salvation of the Lord, which He will accomplish for you today; for the Egyptians whom you have seen today, you will never see them again forever. The Lord will fight for you while you keep silent, Exodus 14:13-14 (NASB)

THE END

Reference

- WorldNet 3.0 Farlex clipart collection © 2003-2012 Princeton University, Farlex Inc.

- Ologies & -Isms. (2008) Gale Group Inc.

www.ingramcontent.com/pod-product-compliance
Lightning Source LLC
Chambersburg PA
CBHW071451040426
42444CB00008B/1292